Teaching Chaucer

Teaching the New English

Published in association with the English Subject Centre
Director: **Ben Knights**

Teaching the New English is an innovative series concerned with the teaching of the English degree in universities in the UK and elsewhere. The series addresses new and developing areas of the curriculum as well as more traditional areas that are reforming in new contexts. Although the Series is grounded in intellectual and theoretical concepts of the curriculum, it is concerned with the practicalities of classroom teaching. The volumes will be invaluable for new and more experienced teachers alike.

Titles include:

Gail Ashton and Louise Sylvester (*editors*)
TEACHING CHAUCER

Charles Butler (*editor*)
TEACHING CHILDREN'S FICTION

Michael Hanrahan and Deborah L. Madsen (*editors*)
TEACHING, TECHNOLOGY, TEXTUALITY
Approaches to New Media

Anna Powell and Andrew Smith (*editors*)
TEACHING THE GOTHIC

Forthcoming titles:

Lisa Hopkins and Andrew Hiscock (*editors*)
TEACHING SHAKESPEARE AND EARLY MODERN DRAMATISTS

Gina Wisker (*editor*)
TEACHING AFRICAN-AMERICAN WOMEN'S WRITING

Teaching the New English
Series Standing Order ISBN 1–4039–4441–5 Hardback 1–4039–4442–3 Paperback
(*outside North America only*)

You can receive future titles in this series as they are published by placing a standing order. Please contact your bookseller or, in case of difficulty, write to us at the address below with your name and address, the title of the series and the ISBN quoted above.

Customer Services Department, Macmillan Distribution Ltd, Houndmills, Basingstoke, Hampshire RG21 6XS, England

Teaching Chaucer

Edited by

Gail Ashton
Lecturer in English, University of Manchester

and

Louise Sylvester
*Senior Lecturer in English, University of Central England
in Birmingham*

First published in 2007 by
PALGRAVE MACMILLAN
Houndmills, Basingstoke, Hampshire RG21 6XS and
175 Fifth Avenue, New York, N.Y. 10010
Companies and representatives throughout the world.

PALGRAVE MACMILLAN is the global academic imprint of the Palgrave
Macmillan division of St. Martin's Press, LLC and of Palgrave Macmillan Ltd.
Macmillan® is a registered trademark in the United States, United Kingdom
and other countries. Palgrave is a registered trademark in the European
Union and other countries.

ISBN-13: 978–1–4039–8826–3 hardback
ISBN-10: 1–4039–8826–9 hardback
ISBN-13: 978–1–4039–8827–0 paperback
ISBN-10: 1–4039–8827–7 paperback

This book is printed on paper suitable for recycling and made from fully
managed and sustained forest sources.

A catalogue record for this book is available from the British Library.

A catalog record for this book is available from the Library of Congress.

10 9 8 7 6 5 4 3 2 1
16 15 14 13 12 11 10 09 08 07

Printed and bound in Great Britain by
Antony Rowe Ltd, Chippenham and Eastbourne

Contents

Series Preface

One of many exciting achievements of the early years of the English Subject Centre was the agreement with Palgrave Macmillan to initiate the series "Teaching the New English." The intention of the then Director, Professor Philip Martin, was to create a series of short and accessible books which would take widely-taught curriculum fields (or, as in the case of learning technologies, approaches to the whole curriculum) and articulate the connections between scholarly knowledge and the demands of teaching.

Since its inception, "English" has been committed to what we know by the portmanteau phrase "learning and teaching." Yet, by and large, university teachers of English—in Britain at all events—find it hard to make their tacit pedagogic knowledge conscious, or to raise it to a level where it might be critiqued, shared, or developed. In the experience of the English Subject Centre, colleagues find it relatively easy to talk about curriculum and resources, but far harder to talk about the success or failure of seminars, how to vary forms of assessment, or to make imaginative use of Virtual Learning Environments. Too often this reticence means falling back on received assumptions about student learning, about teaching, or about forms of assessment. At the same time, colleagues are often suspicious of the insights and methods arising from generic educational research. The challenge for the English group of disciplines is therefore to articulate ways in which our own subject knowledge and ways of talking might themselves refresh debates about pedagogy. The implicit invitation of this series is to take fields of knowledge and survey them through a pedagogic lens. Research and scholarship, and teaching and learning are part of the same process, not two separate domains.

"Teachers," people used to say, "are born not made." There may, after all, be some tenuous truth in this: there may be generosities of spirit (or, alternatively, drives for didactic control) laid down in earliest childhood. But why should we assume that even "born" teachers (or novelists, or nurses, or veterinary surgeons) do not need to learn the skills of their trade? Amateurishness about teaching has far more to do with university claims to status, than with evidence about how people learn. There is a craft to shaping and promoting learning. This series of books is dedicated to the development of the craft of teaching within English Studies.

Ben Knights
Teaching the New English *Series Editor*
Director, English Subject Centre
Higher Education Academy

The English Subject Centre

Founded in 2000, the English Subject Centre (which is based at Royal Holloway, University of London) is part of the subject network of the Higher Education Academy. Its purpose is to develop learning and teaching across the English disciplines in UK Higher Education. To this end it engages in research and publication (web and print), hosts events and conferences, sponsors projects, and engages in day-to-day dialogue with its subject communities.

http://www.english.heacademy.ac.uk

Acknowledgements

We are grateful to the contributors to this volume for their wonderful and lively projects and for writing about their teaching in such engaging ways. We are also grateful for their incredible helpfulness in accommodating a schedule which occasionally demanded work from them at short notice. We should also like to thank Stewart Brookes for his editorial assistance in the final stages of the project.

Gail Ashton
Louise Sylvester
March 2006

Notes on the Contributors

Gail Ashton is Lecturer in Medieval Literature and Culture at the University of Manchester. Her research and teaching interests range from Chaucer to queer and gender theories, contemporary female novelists and creative writing. She is especially interested in electronic media and in how students learn. She has published books and articles on Chaucer, female hagiography and romance.

Lesley Coote is Lecturer in English and Film Studies at the University of Hull. Her main research interests are prophecy and politics from the Middle Ages to the early modern period, Arthurian and romance epic and medievalist film. She is particularly interested in making medieval text accessible through the visual (static and moving) image, and the part which may be played by digital and "new media" in this process. A university teaching fellow and associate of the university's Centre for Learning Development, she is currently undertaking a research project in the development of valid criteria for the use of innovative and creative assessment methods in the English honours degree curriculum.

Moira Fitzgibbons is Assistant Professor in the English Department at Marist College. Her scholarly interests include: depictions of intellectual and imaginative activity in late medieval popular religion; women's spirituality and reading practices; Chaucer; pedagogical theories, both medieval and modern.

Simon Horobin is Reader in English Language at the University of Glasgow. He has research and teaching interests in medieval English language and literature and is the author of *The Language of the Chaucer Tradition* (2003).

Peggy A. Knapp is Professor of English at Carnegie Mellon University, Pittsburgh, Pennsylvania. She writes about and teaches courses on medieval and renaissance texts, but also on contemporary literary theory and aesthetics. Her books include *Chaucer and the Social Contest* (1990) and *Time-Bound Words: Semantic and Social Economies from Chaucer's England to Shakespeare's* (2000), and she is currently working on Chaucerian Aesthetics.

Steven F. Kruger is Professor of English and Medieval Studies at Queens College and the Graduate Center of the City University of New York. His most recent book is *The Spectral Jew: Conversion and Embodiment in Medieval Europe* (2006), and he continues to work on medieval interreligious interactions.

Philippa Semper is Lecturer in Medieval English Language and Literature at the University of Birmingham. Her research examines the relationships between text and image in medieval manuscripts, the various reading strategies required by differing forms of visual exposition, and the implications of such strategies for both the production and the use of manuscripts. She is interested in e-learning and the development of web-based learning materials and is currently Director of Learning and Teaching for the School of Humanities at Birmingham.

Louise Sylvester is Senior Lecturer in English at the University of Central England, Birmingham. Her main research interest concerns the construction of meaning from the level of the word upwards. She has published books and essays on word studies in Middle English and cognitive approaches to the construction of lexicographical resources as well as articles on reading rape in medieval literature.

Fiona Tolhurst is Associate Professor of English at Alfred University, New York. She has published articles on medieval Arthurian literature in a variety of journals and has contributed to volumes such as *Eleanor of Aquitaine: Lord and Lady* and *Re-Viewing Le Morte Darthur*. Her current research interests include C. S. Lewis's Arthurian connections and Geoffrey of Monmouth's *Historia Regum Britanniae*. Her teaching interests include medieval and modern Arthurian literature, Chaucer, the Middle Ages in literature and film, and women writers of the Middle Ages.

Introduction

Gail Ashton

Introduction

The *New Chaucer Society*'s colloquium on teaching Chaucer that was inaugurated in Dublin in 1994 is now a regular event. The New York meeting in 2006 had a panel on pedagogical issues, organised by Larry Benson, and was open to teachers in schools and colleges as well as universities. The present volume of essays springs from a panel presentation and discussion on innovations in Chaucer teaching that Louise Sylvester and I organised for the *New Chaucer Society* in Glasgow in 2004. Implicit within its rationale was the question of how far pedagogical theories and practices have moved in the intervening years and it is here that I would like to begin.

In her introduction to the collection of papers that emerged from that 1994 meeting, Christine Rose identifies the state of Chaucer teaching in the 1990s. Her list of the concerns common to teachers of Chaucer include the following: the place of Chaucer in a shrinking course catalogue; the effects of historical and cultural difference; how to integrate theoretical scholarship into teaching; the need to respond to a restructuring of course provision according to the principles of cross-genre, cross-period and interdisciplinarity; and a diminishing, even resistant, literacy in Middle English and medieval contexts more generally (Rose 1996: 3). Then, as now, the near-impossibility of negotiating all of these issues in a single semester, or less, is the driving force of our teaching. I would certainly agree with Rose that, despite this, so many Chaucer teachers continue to devise stimulating courses for their students, often leading the way in an innovation partly borne of the necessity of responding to the dwindling take-up of medieval literature (Rose 1996: 3).

At first glance, it seems then that little has changed. There is, however, one crucial difference. In 1994, Rose speaks of the "teacher-scholars" and "master-teachers" who contributed to that forum (Rose 1996: 1). It is precisely this top-down, authoritative model of the teacher disseminating a body of knowledge (scholarship) that has shifted. *This* collection explores the notion of teacher as guide, facilitating a hands-on supported learning that takes place *in dialogue* with active learners. Some of our contributors directly confront this move (Ashton, Coote, Fitzgibbons). *All* engage it at some point to reflect on the sorts of activities we expect our students *to do*, the concomitant changes in styles of teaching and in the methods of assessment we construct.

Rose also comments on what she perceives as the happy marriage of academic research and investment in teaching and learning (Rose 1996: 2). One of the threads of my own discussion is the sense that Rose's optimism was misplaced and that the alliance is far from unproblematic. That said, there are signs of a more positive commitment to the integration of these two crucial activities: external and in-house financial support for innovative projects, investigations and career development; the establishment of a national English Subject Centre, based at Royal Holloway, University of London, Centres of Excellence for teaching throughout the UK and of fully supported National Teaching Fellowships; the proliferation of pedagogical journals and the inclusion of such research in the Research Assessment Exercise 2008; and so on. In this more welcoming environment, perhaps what Rose hoped for over ten years ago might finally begin to come about.

Contexts

A glance at our list of contributors reveals the diversity of their backgrounds and interests. Our authors work in the UK in research-led redbrick universities and post-1992 institutions like the University of Central England, and in liberal arts colleges and large state universities in the US. Their essays mainly centre on undergraduate teaching (except Horobin and Knapp) and, save for the two in which the focus is on language, on teaching Chaucer to students of literature. Their work sets up cross-currents and a cross-pollination of ideas to speak in dialogue to and amongst each other, hence the lack of a summarising introduction; we would rather readers dip in and read across articles as well as selecting those of personal interest.

Here, and in the classroom, probably the most crucial factor influencing what we teach, and how, is the context of our particular environments.

We all begin by taking into account class size; the logistics of timetabling; aims and outcomes; whether a course is optional, compulsory, introductory, survey, or specialised stand-alone; and its place in a wider programme provision. We can and do respond to these external impositions in a variety of flexible and interesting ways, but we can't begin to design our courses until we have accounted for their contexts. Of course, we all make value judgements and philosophical choices when we teach. My intention in reminding us of some of those approaches that are unique to teachers of Chaucer, is an attempt to make them available for scrutiny and to stimulate further debate about the ways in which we might continue to negotiate them.

To some extent, the main divide appears to be between those who privilege a theoretical and critical study of Chaucer and those "pure" historicists who explore his works as a medieval cultural phenomenon (see Knapp, Kruger, Tolhurst, this volume). Interestingly, none of the essays in our volume directly discusses the former. It is as though this approach has become the new orthodoxy in Chaucer Studies, an assumption that we would do well to scrutinise further. Equally, others deploy manuscript evidence or the study of language (Horobin and Knapp), a context more readily available than in the past, thanks to the Internet and a wealth of electronic resources and projects. Some approach Chaucer through performance (Fitzgibbons, Tolhurst) and collaborative learning-as-process (Ashton, Coote, Fitzgibbons, Horobin, Kruger, Tolhurst), with the aim of allowing students some responsibility for their own learning. Others structure and deliver learning through electronic mediums (Ashton, Coote, Semper) or else use a building block model of learning, guiding and supporting students through bite-sized research tasks (Horobin, Knapp, Kruger, Semper, Coote). Above all, many teachers mix these approaches and keep in play a tension between the alterity of Chaucer and his continuities with our own time that is not unique to Chaucer Studies.

It does, though, promise "an important site for its exploration" (Field 2005: 13), a challenge that we would do well to take further if we are to continue to influence students' perceptions, provoke questions and side-step the demands of goal-oriented, passive learners. In the age of student-as-consumer, this is sometimes an unwelcome or uneasy negotiation. And so we need, once more, to think through and clarify our agendas. What do we teach: the *Canterbury Tales* or other texts, and which editions, printed or on-line? Theory or history or both? What sorts of questions do we want our students to engage and to ask of themselves? What are our hopes and visions? Are our conflicting approaches to Chaucer a danger or key to his survival in academia? And if we do want to retain this plurality, to do *everything* in one short time, then how best might we create effective learning environments?

Even the briefest consideration of the nuts and bolts of our classrooms reveals some of the ways in which our choices as teachers actively shape and construct Chaucer Studies in equal measure to the kinds of research and scholarship we undertake. We need to ask to which resources do we guide students? How do we compile reading lists and what kinds of critical material do we use? Possibly one of the most overlooked questions is which Chaucer texts do we study?

Rosalind Field's survey of Chaucer teachers in the UK indicates that the *Tales* is our first-choice text. We seem, too, to be heavily reliant on tales like the Miller's, the Wife's, and the Pardoner's, as well as the *General Prologue* (Field 2005: 10). One of the most obvious consequences of this packaging of Chaucer is that it encourages a limiting world-view of him as simply a bawdy comedian. Less clear is the unarticulated assumption of shared values that lies behind these selections. Is it pragmatic, a decision to "sell" fun or accessible tales as part of the ways in which students might be encouraged to confront close reading of difficult or different texts? This emphasis upon the *Canterbury Tales* implicates too the afterlife of poems like *Troilus and Criseyde* or the *Legend of Good Women*, an issue taken up by Tolhurst in this volume. We need to air the possibility that the effect of our preferences, intentionally or otherwise, sidelines Chaucer's other works, or even imbues them with a sense that only these are worthy of committed, specialist study, a manoeuvre that, in the long term, further isolates Chaucer Studies.

This dichotomy is also embedded in the increasing gap between study guides to Chaucer or introductory critical texts and academic scholarship, a gulf that widens in the face of institutional disparagement of the former in spite of the considerable research investment and writing expertise they demand. Field calls for more "high-quality, scholarly works of general applicability" to mediate this divide (Field 2005: 10), but this important interface of research/teaching still lacks sufficient esteem or adequate reward. Perhaps another way forward might be to integrate introductory guides with more academic material, to offer a series of starting points and questions that invite critical analysis and reflection on *both*.

Chaucer as living tradition

The creation of any learning environment is coloured as much by what our students bring to our classrooms as by our own particular ethos. It is often the case that students are drawn to medieval courses by awareness, however slight, of a culture they erroneously construct from contemporary and popular sources. The range of material is vast. Peter Ackroyd's *Clerkenwell Tales* (2003) is Chaucerian in spirit only. So, too, *A Knight's Tale* (2001) which features a naked Chaucer and breaks all the rules of medieval "estate." Jonathan Myerson's animated BBC TV *Tales* presents a palatable Chaucer delivered in both modern and Middle English (1998–2000), while BBC1's series of contemporary "writing-back" takes six tales to produce some interesting new versions (2003). The Royal Shakespeare Company presents the complete *Canterbury Tales* (seemingly save for the *Melibee*) at the Swan Theatre, Stratford-upon-Avon (2005), before taking it on a nationwide UK tour (2006).

However welcome this initial sparking of interest might be, many versions of Chaucer circulating in popular culture do tend to give the impression that "the story of the Middle Ages is one long *fabliau*" (Remley 1996: 32), something our selection of "set" poems from the *Canterbury Tales* often aggravates. It is sometimes difficult to strike a balance between an accessible "showcase" Chaucer and one that satisfies the demands of academic rigour. My own view is that anything that has students sign up for our courses, from where we can then offer a taste of "the real thing" (Camargo 2005: 246), is a bonus. We might also use these early impressions as a starting point for dialogue. One of my openers on the electronic discussion board asks what students expect from this course and what they currently "know" about Chaucer. Sharing these perceptions allows teachers to address these issues in seminar discussions, lectures, through questions and activities, and through the readings to which we direct our students. In other words, we can construct units of study *in conversation* with students, working out from their own experiences and prejudices and actively countering them, rather than imposing answers and critical "truths." We must also remember that Field's study of Chaucer teaching testifies to the continuing popularity of Chaucer, once students overcome their initial tendencies towards reluctance and anxiety about an author whom most have never studied before and who writes in an unfamiliar language (Field 2005: 4).

Teachers of Chaucer ultimately face many demands upon their resourcefulness. It seems that either students don't want to "do" Chaucer at first, or else they expect only the bawdy comedy of popular Chaucer. There is also a certain ambivalence amongst many teachers who, on the one hand, struggle to "correct" these assumptions, and, on the other, believe that prior study of Chaucer at AS and A2 level (still the

predominant entry route into higher education in the UK) actively dis-
advantages students, presumably because of the conservative approaches
encouraged by our examination systems (Field 2005: 5). In universities
and colleges, Chaucer is increasingly offered as either a stand-alone
example of medieval literature and culture, or as part of a compulsory
survey or introductory course. Both occur early on in the degree programmes of many institutions. These usually first year undergraduate
modules are often our only chance to advertise Chaucer in preparation
for later specialist options. Yet it is also the point of entry at which our
student uptake is likely to be most diverse. At the same time, there is an
inherent problematic in using Chaucer as a snapshot of medieval culture. Of course, he is highly adaptable and responsive to a range of
approaches; in the process he becomes accessible and up to date, especially given his poetry's pliability in the face of gendered or other theoretical manoeuvres, such as post-colonial and eco readings. Yet, this very
modernisation also risks detaching Chaucer's work from its medieval
context, at exactly the same time as he remains peculiarly *"unmedieval"*
(Field 2005: 7). It certainly seems timely for us to revisit this practice and
to consider further some of the issues arising from Chaucer's continued
afterlife, both in and outside our higher education settings.

Elaine Tuttle Hansen is concerned that confining Chaucer Studies to
the higher echelons of education will give us a cachet of sophisticated
readers and active graduates that, nevertheless, misses "the large numbers of more underprepared, more difficult-to-teach college students
who are less interested in reading" (Hansen 2005: 286). Hansen maybe
overstates her case; many of the essays in this volume bear witness to
some lively and innovative teaching in sometimes difficult circumstances (see especially Coote, Fitzgibbons, Kruger). Yet, paradoxically,
the danger she identifies may be more acute than ever. The thorny issue
of Middle English is pivotal here. More generally, we sometimes
threaten to disappear behind a cultural divide, aided and abetted by a
"publish or die" pressure that enforces academic specialisation and
leaves Chaucer Studies stranded, to become simply elitist and bookish.

A way to negotiate this potential impasse, and to ensure that Chaucer
thrives, is to take him out into schools and colleges of further education.
Colloquia like Steve Ellis's "Teaching Chaucer Today" (Birmingham,
June 2005) bring together higher education and school teachers to share
good practice and try to build a "productive, fruitful" interface between
the academy and a culture "at large" (Ellis 2000: 165). At the same time,
they demonstrate "the vitality of Chaucer teaching" at all levels, often
"in the face of all institutional obstacles" (Gibson 2005). Projects that

focus on digital images and visual media (Coote, this volume), on reading aloud and/or performance of Chaucer's works (Fitzgibbons, Tolhurst), CD-ROMs of performances or related material, electronic audio clips of Middle English, and creative writing projects—such as the competition accompanying BBC TV's 2003 adaptations of Chaucer—all actively contribute to a vigorous afterlife that we would do well to nurture. A heavily stratified education system that still prioritises a print medium and the academic research of the lone scholar plays its own part in skewing perceptions of Chaucer by suppressing a group dynamic, the oral and performative aspects of his works. This is, after all, vernacular poetry. It adapts and tells stories, most of them not original. Some are incomplete. All of them require and respond to an audience. Why then are we not thinking about more fluid, tentative, collaborative projects and building-in assessments that mingle product (written exam or essay) *and* process (portfolio, workshop, outcomes in forms other than written)? After all, no one can perform, modernise, translate, adapt or otherwise "write-back" unless they have already engaged an original. These are possibilities that all of our contributors confront in various ways. Steve Ellis asks "whose loss will it be if fifty years from now Chaucer remains known outside the academy only as the mouthpiece of an uncomplicated bawdy affability" (Ellis 2000: 163); we have both the answer and the means, if only we could open up a dialogue between our ivory towers and the world out there.

A question of language

The impetus for what follows is Lee Patterson's provocation that "no-one can teach Chaucer without also teaching how to read and pronounce Middle English accurately" (Patterson 1996: 20). In an era of easy access to those on-line modernisations that, as teachers, we ignore at our peril, Patterson's declaration—in reality, a clarion call for a particular ideological approach—is demonstrably untrue. Yet the question of which language, authentic Middle English or contemporary idiomatic translation, clearly remains a dilemma for most of us. I suggest that it is not the simple binary it appears; instead, it foregrounds other assumptions and issues about Chaucer Studies that, in turn, impact upon our teaching.

Writing as part of a *Studies in the Age of Chaucer* colloquium on the welfare of Chaucer Studies, Martin Camargo wonders how much longer he can go on teaching Chaucer "as a poet, while pretending that even the very best of my students are regularly reading his works in the original Middle English" (Camargo 2005: 246). For some, the decision to allow students to use translations is a pragmatic one. Paul Remley acknowledges personal misgivings even as he promotes their use, arguing that there is little room for choice when teaching large class sizes of disparate students in a condensed time frame (Remley 1996: 33). Some believe, too, that it may be better to read Chaucer in translation than not at all. Yet many others remain committed to engaging students with Middle English and do so in a variety of interesting ways, as a large number of our contributors demonstrate.

In his review of David Wright's 1980s prose translation of the *Canterbury Tales* (1987), Derek Pearsall observes that only a reading in Middle English can help in understanding Chaucer and "his" English (cited in Ellis 2000: 200), adding that those using translations rarely proceed to the originals. Several essays in this volume also offer a spirited rationale in support of Pearsall's view (see especially Kruger and Knapp). But Chaucer continues to present particular difficulties to literature students who are presented with an English they do not immediately recognise. Many of those will have little previous study experience of Chaucer, a factor possibly exacerbated by his increasing lack of visibility in the pedagogical structures of schools and colleges. Indeed, this perceived linguistic difficulty may well partially account for Chaucer's slippage into the optional elements of post-16 AS and A2 level English examinations and his omission from the National Curriculum, where he is superseded by an iconic, compulsory and status-laden Shakespeare. At the same time, it seems that virtually all of us, if not already teaching Chaucer in Middle English in higher education, wish that we could.

There are a number of problematics embedded within the debate I have only briefly sketched here. The first is an assumption that Chaucer's Middle English is a static, gold standard similar enough to modern Englishes to warrant citation of an "original" language which was, in fact, not shared by his contemporaries. Sylvester's research (this volume) suggests that whereas Chaucer is often taught through the medium of Middle English, other medieval authors are taught in translation. Sylvester also points out that teachers of Chaucer tend to make reading in Middle English a requirement of their courses without necessarily fully considering how this will come about. Often, reading and translation exercises take up an introductory part of a course (if at all) before being overtaken by historical, cultural, and theoretical concerns. Students who lack familiarity with and competency in Middle English structures—notably those on survey or introductory courses—are unlikely to continue to improve unless more, and continuous, explicit attention is given to language. (See Horobin, Knapp and Kruger in this collection for ideas on how to ameliorate this.) Where this is simply not feasible, should we abandon the attempt altogether?

Equally, a demographic largely composed of literature students and teachers may approach issues of language entirely differently from linguistic experts. In this sense, to assume an authentic originality for *Chaucer's* Middle English—what Pearsall paternalistically cites as "his" English in the example quoted earlier—is, at best, misleading and possibly dishonest. Even within Chaucer's own poetry, Middle English is a slippery construct, a factor that a generally consistent use of the Riverside package as a set text persistently ignores. One teacher's call for an exchange of ideas on teaching Middle English specifically to literature students, in Field's study of Chaucer teaching in UK universities (Field 2005: 13), is clearly timely, as is Sylvester's consideration of the implications of dividing language and literature from each other in our course provision (this volume). Rather than insisting on a word by word understanding of Middle English, maybe we ought instead to emphasise the transmission and reception of manuscripts and texts, and of Chaucer as an author, as a means of engaging with language issues in a considered historical and cultural frame (see Horobin, this volume).

Another important issue is the use of translations. I commend those who regularly incorporate reading in both Middle and modern English; but is it helpful when the premise is to highlight the "inadequacies of any translation" (Goodman 1996: 10)? It may well be that foregoing Middle English contributes to Chaucer's continued neglect, certainly outside the academy (Ellis 2000: 99). This is particularly the case with abbreviated or otherwise poor modernisations. Steve Ellis scorns, for example, the modern "half" of BBC TV's animated *Tales* (1988–2000) for reducing "the text to a series of blunt formulations" (Ellis 2000: 140). Concern about the poetic or literary value of translations is entirely justified. It is, though, not the same as a blanket condemnation of all translations, seen in some of the major players in Chaucer Studies who abhor anything other than the original. The lack of translations by reputable poets, correctly identified by Steve Ellis in his *Chaucer At Large* (Ellis 2000: 94), undoubtedly hinders genuine progress, even, debate, as far as this issue is concerned. It may be timely to remind ourselves of the differences between translations and modernisations or web-resourced cribs *and* of the inherent stumbling block in translating Chaucer well: the fact that his language may seem like our own. A good translation will offer a "root-and-branch renewal" (Ellis 2000: 100), the "performance of one text in a new language, rather than a carbon copy of the original in a different one" (Ellis 2002: 443), an enterprise that is, after all, remarkably Chaucerian.

We need, then, to reconsider not whether we use translations but, rather, what kinds of translations might be acceptable. It would, I think, be productive to take up Ellis's challenge to begin exploring the practice of translation, celebrating it as a "textual adventure" in its own right (Ellis 2000: 120 and 100). At the same time, we might encourage critical responses to them amongst our students, perhaps making this part of an assessed in-class exercise or independent research project. That said, as ever, context is all; in deciding how best to approach these issues, we must always consider our own unique learning environments and the sorts of students we encounter on our courses. One thing is sure: our stubborn refusal to grapple seriously with the question of Middle English impacts upon the sorts of scholarship with which we want our students to converse. Translations speak to a network of relations that constitute medieval authorship. As such, the ambivalent status of translations is part of that same hermeneutic web. It is not good enough to sneer at contemporary translations as inferior to the originals, or as separate from the "real" study of Chaucer which increasingly becomes the property of our graduate or high achieving students. They are "part of that nexus of commentary and exegesis on a source text" and so deserving of study in their own right (Ellis 2000: 165). In short, our dilemma may not be Coghill *or* Chaucer, but how best to integrate the two and sow the seeds for a future rendition of the *Canterbury Tales* equal in stature to Seamus Heaney's *Beowulf*.

E-learning and web-based resources

If technological forms of communication are the new literacy, then, perhaps, there is a case for ensuring that departments of English are at the forefront of a movement that looks set to redefine the ways we share ideas and "make" texts. It seems fitting that just as Chaucer was writing at the intersection of print and oral cultures in the late fourteenth century, so, too, Chaucer Studies must negotiate a similarly revolutionary dynamic in the twenty-first. Many higher education practitioners, medievalists in particular, have already responded proactively to the opportunities inherent in various forms of e-learning, those at Birmingham, Hull, Glasgow and Manchester to name but a few. The English Subject Centre (Royal Holloway, University of London) continues to engender initiatives in the technologies of teaching and learning. It supports projects and conferences, while its Learning Technology Officer and Website Developer, currently Brett Lucas, has a regular column in the Centre's Newsletters that rounds up teaching-related developments in IT (see http://www.english.heacademy.ac.uk/explore/publications/index.php). Similarly, the Joint Information Systems Committee (JISC) has published an e-Learning guide on CD-ROM, "Innovative Practice with e-learning" (http://www.jisc.ac.uk/eli_practice.html).

There are numerous advantages in using web-resourced or e-learning instead of, or alongside, traditional classroom-based contexts. A fully supported electronic learning environment can provide off-campus, 24/7, open access to all registered students, plus a variety of resources: "gist" or bite-sized tasters for background or contextual information; links to other websites and resources as well as bibliographies; digital images and electronic facsimiles of manuscript or other material evidence; on-line editions of Chaucer's works in modern and/or Middle English; electronic discussion forums and virtual classrooms complete with quizzes, exercises and fully supported independent and collaborative research topics; interactive and value-added lectures (those with preparatory and follow-up activities); and all the course information students will need located in one easily accessible place. The flexibility of these features goes some way towards satisfying the many and often apparently conflicting demands that seem to come with the territory of Chaucer Studies and which I discussed earlier. An added benefit is an ability to create a genuine learning community for those especially large or disparate cohorts of students (see Ashton, Coote and Semper, this volume). At the same time, an electronic learning environment allows us to build an ongoing, expanding resource *and* automatically archive its material and interactions so that students and teachers might retrieve it for evaluation and reflection. Above all, in integrating such a facility, we engage the four primary processes commonly identified as the means through which students learn best. That is, they can work at their own pace, in a time and location of their choice, control their own learning to some extent, and, often negotiate it through the assistance of their peers (Broad et al. 2004: 139).

There is, though, a danger that an ill-considered move to learning environments where technological communication is its main component simply becomes "a coat-hanger where files are left for students to access" (Broad et al. 2004: 149). As well as offering "distributed access to a seamless network of course materials and relevant information sources" (Broad et al. 2004: 136), it demands a shift of focus to student-centred learning. No longer the authoritative owner of knowledge, teachers must become, instead, facilitators working with students whose role also alters; they must now take active responsibility for their own learning and invest in a course that is no longer provided top-down.

The context, design and presentation of such courses require considerable effort in terms of time and energy, and, also, a commitment to a continuous process of reflection. Broad advises of the need to consider "the perspective of the authors and learners . . . as well as the learning culture of the student" (Broad et al. 2004: 139). In this respect, the demands are no different from those of any other course unit, but there are some unique potential traps for the inexperienced.

The rationale behind the creation of any course is surely to enhance student learning. It is sometimes tempting for management to ignore this and support the use of a Virtual Learning Environment (VLE) as a means of alleviating academic pressures by reducing contact time accordingly and promoting distance learning. We should be wary of such conflicts of interest and note that web learning appears to work most effectively when it is *not* a replacement for real-life teaching, or used as a panacea for all institutional problems. Semper's experience of web-based learning suggests that those students who use it most productively are already highly motivated to do so, possibly because they are familiar with its techniques. As a result, they are the ones best placed to construct networks of ideas and synthesise material in ways that reflect deep, rather than surface, learning. Other students have different learning preferences and may want more, not less, hands-on human intervention (Semper, this volume). Over-reliance on e-learning also leads to fatigue amongst learners who reduce their input accordingly. For teachers, too, there are pitfalls. Diana Laurillard points out that if we only "introduce learning technologies . . . on an experimental pilot basis," then students will not perceive them as being as serious as other forms of learning. Instead, teachers "must build on the work done and follow it through;" above all, all electronic work ought to be assessed (Laurillard 2002: 205).

This question of assessment is a difficult one. To always grade the work that students do with electronic media panders to a goal-oriented culture that seems anathema to the free-flowing dialogue and interconnections of the web. Equally, it may lead to a series of sterile, even purely quantitative, exercises. Certainly, the demands of this type of learning are different from the familiar environment of real classrooms; accordingly, we need to rethink forms and kinds of assessment, to take into account collaborative and group learning as well as independent work. A more flexible approach might also be to make it part of a raft of assessment choices more closely matched to the "best practice" use of e-learning. Thus we need to consider a range of specific contexts and teaching and learning styles, as a means of enhancing the *processes* of learning and its outcomes. Such technologies can never replace traditional teaching. Rather, they work most efficiently in a form of blended learning that permits students choice and independence, yet supports their efforts, that integrates face-to-face and virtual contexts, and selects from a range of web-based resources to produce learning environments that are adaptable, stimulating, user-friendly and, above all, different every time.

Afterthoughts

Martin Camargo calls for "tireless advocacy" in promoting and preserving medieval studies. His recommendation that teachers working in the field ought to connect with each other, in and out and across higher education institutions, is suggestive, given this volume's emphasis upon continuous dialogue (Camargo 2005: 247). I would like to add to that my own hope that we participate in a series of exchanges: with our students, with the texts we select for their reading *and* those we choose to write, and with the wealth of learning strategies and teaching technologies that come to us from a range of subject disciplines and areas. In so doing, we need to reconsider the whys and hows of our teaching, thinking about the kinds of frameworks we construct for our courses and the contexts in which active learning might take place. This also means reviewing opportunities for the different kinds of assessment that many of these units of study demand, taking care to resist pressure to homogenise course provision or fall back upon familiar options, such as coursework assignments and traditional examination. Above all, we must be prepared to abandon, when appropriate, our traditional role as authoritative "knower," to "look less to our notes, and more to our students and the text" (Hagen 1996: 7). As Susan Hagen noted as long ago as 1996, this shift from master class expert to learning facilitator demands an openness and flexibility that means "We have to be ready not just for what we want to do but for just about anything. It is not an anxiety free way to teach" (Hagen 1996: 6).

We hope that the essays in this collection demonstrate that crucial to our successes as teachers is outstanding scholarship combined with innovative teaching (Camargo 2005: 247). Certainly, they feed into that nexus of explorations and conversations already emerging in recent impulses to revalue pedagogy; that is, to bring it out of the darkness of the peripheral and into the light of serious, evaluated consideration as something integral to academic development. There are already signs of progress in this enterprise. Palgrave Macmillan's *Teaching the New English* essay collections, of which this volume is part, promises much, as do the English Subject Centre's ongoing compilations of good practice guides and case studies in innovation. (For more details, see http://www.english.heacademy.ac.uk/explore/publications/newenglish.php and http://www.english.heacademy.ac.uk/explore/publications/case-studies.php.) As suggested earlier, many journals devoted to pedagogical theories and practices are beginning to engage teachers of English, while numerous conferences contribute to an emerging discussion. Here, Royal Holloway's "Renewals: Refiguring University English in the Twenty-First Century" (Royal Holloway, University of London, 2007 July 5–7) taps into a current and prevalent ethos, planning for reflections, presentations and workshops to explore the ways students and teachers "do" English, and to enable experiences and expertise of all kinds to "enter into dialogue" (http://www.english. heacademy.ac.uk/renewals).

There is, however, no doubt that at present this dialogue remains a tentative and conflicted one. Most UK universities have responded by providing training for new and incumbent academics. Sometimes this is compulsory or allied to probation or tenure. Yet, according to a study by Gibbs and Coffey, in practice its provision is often insubstantial and/or of variable quality (2004: 88–9), even though staff development is a serious concern. Student-focused teaching doesn't simply "happen." Rather, it calls for considerable investment in terms of time, planning, skills, and creativity. Neither is it the only strategy for effective learning. In this case, we need a careful programme of training that enables us to become conversant with a range of approaches if we are to offer varied, stimulating, effective learning environments for our students.

One of the ways this might be negotiated is through the creation of "an intellectually rigorous tradition (or traditions) of writing about teaching" that moves away from a social-science based discourse and towards a more "English-specific" one (Gibson 2005). Ben Knights, Director of the English Subject Centre based at Royal Holloway, rightly remarks the difficulties many teachers of English experience when called upon to write or talk about how they work with students, or to make taken-for-granted assumptions and practices "available to others or even to ourselves for scrutiny" (Knights 2005: 2). Many of us contributing to this volume would, I think, endorse these comments and point to an ambivalence that leaves us able to describe the nuts and bolts of our projects with ease; far more problematic is the process of reflection, especially in the absence of established models of scholarship that speak directly to and for the particular experiences of those working in the humanities. This volume, and others like it, is testament to the importance of overcoming these anxieties and of making our voices heard in an ongoing and *inclusive* debate.

My wish list for the enabling of reflective, skilled and flexible practitioners goes further. A call for more conferences, the submission of more articles to reputable pedagogic journals and an ongoing exchange of good practice shared in a discourse of our own must be matched by academic approval and recognition in the academic institutions in which we work. This means more transparent and equitable rewards for the promotion of excellence in teaching, including investment in training and in mentoring schemes for *all* teachers, and in teams of Learning Practitioners to support technological and other innovation. It may well be that a way forward is to make compulsory the acquisition of a formally accredited PGCE in Higher Education, as is currently the case for school and college teachers. Perhaps, too, we ought to reconsider the practice of pitching inexperienced graduate and doctoral students into teaching at the same time as they are writing a thesis and seeking to establish a publications record. It is, after all, erroneous to assume that their teaching will be student-centred simply because they retain a student perspective on learning. I am not attempting to decry the valuable and often only semi-visible work that graduate teaching assistants achieve, often without adequate preparation and support. My concern is a potential clash of impulses: that of the skills-trained version of the lone scholar set against the open, student-focused teacher.

Of course, the issues I raise impact upon teachers of English everywhere, not just those working in Chaucer Studies or a medieval field. But here, too, some of my comments have especial significance. Evidence suggests that Chaucer often occupies a unique place in Year 1 undergraduate course provision, including compulsory survey and core modules. Often this is our opportunity to "showcase" this author and his works. In which case, the practice of many UK universities of devolving such teaching to Ph.D. students may well prove short-sighted. At the same time, our advocacy of the amorphous and shifting area we term "Chaucer Studies" does not stop at the university door. Perhaps, we would do well to consider and debate the complex interrelations of university and school *curricula*, of academic Chaucer and the versions circulating outside those circles in popular culture, if we are to ensure a flourishing afterlife for Chaucer's poems.

Works cited

Ackroyd, Peter (2003). *The Clerkenwell Tales*. London: Chatto & Windus

Broad, Martin, Marian Matthews, & Andrew McDonald (2004). "Active Learning in Higher Education", *Accounting Education Through an Online-Supported Virtual Learning Environment*, 5.2: 135–51

Camargo, Martin (2005). "The State of Medieval Studies: A Tale of Two Universities", *Studies in the Age of Chaucer*, 27: 239–47

Coghill, Nevill (1960). *The Canterbury Tales Translated into Modern English*. London: Penguin

Ellis, Roger (2002). "Translation", in *Companion*, ed. Brown. Oxford: Blackwell: pp. 443–58

Ellis, Steve (2000). *Chaucer at Large: The Poet in the Popular Imagination*. Minneapolis: University of Minnesota Press

Field, Rosalind (2005). *Chaucer Teaching in UK Universities*: http://www.oup.com/uk/booksites/content/0199259127/resources/ukuniversities. pdf

Gibbs, Graham & Martin Coffey (2004). "The Impact of Training of University Teachers on their Teaching Skills, their Approaches to Teaching and the Approach to Learning of their Students", *Active Learning in Higher Education*, 5.1: 87–101

Gibson, Jonathan (2005). "Pedagogic Research in English", *English Subject Centre Newsletter*, 9

Goodman, Thomas (1996). "On Literacy", *Exemplaria* (Teaching Chaucer in the 90s), 8.2: 459–72

Hagen, Susan K. (1996). "Interdisciplinary Chaucer", *Exemplaria* (Teaching Chaucer in the 90s): http://web.english.ufl.edu/exemplaria/sympo. html#hagen

Hansen, Elaine T. (2005). "Response: Chaucerian Values", *Studies in the Age of Chaucer*, 27: 277–87

Heaney, Seamus (1999). *Beowulf*. London: Faber

A Knight's Tale, dir. Brian Helgeland. Columbia Pictures, 2001

Knights, Ben (2005). "Foreword", *English Subject Centre Newsletter*, 9: 2–3

Laurillard, Diana (2002). *Rethinking University Teaching and Learning: A Conversational Framework for the Effective Use of Learning Technologies*. London: RoutledgeFalmer

Patterson, Lee (1996). "The Disenchanted Classroom", *Exemplaria* (Teaching Chaucer in the 90s): http://web.english.ufl.edu/exemplaria/sympo.html#patterson

Remley, Paul (1996). "Questions of Subjectivity and Ideology in the Production of an Electronic Text of the *Canterbury Tales*", *Exemplaria* (Teaching Chaucer in the 90s): http://web.english.ufl.edu/exemplaria/sympo.html#remley

Rose, Christine (1996). "Introduction to Teaching Chaucer in the 90s", *Exemplaria* (Teaching Chaucer in the 90s): http://web.english.ufl.edu/ exemplaria/sympo.html#rose

1
Chaucer for Fun and Profit

Peggy A. Knapp

The experience of studying the *Canterbury Tales* (the text on which I will concentrate in this essay) involves historical discovery, philosophical seriousness, emotional engagement, and, often, spontaneous laughter. A good deal of historical groundwork is necessary to prevent this many-faceted text from being a mere relic from the past, charming perhaps, but quaint. Such historical inquiry itself affords the pleasure of intuiting how the tales speak to one another, to the fiction as a whole, and to the culture from and for which the text was first written. Yet the philosophical issues it raises, often lightheartedly, are still being pondered, though in somewhat different formulations. Attention to the *Canterbury Tales* as art discloses even more immediate pleasures, since art seems to defy time, facing readers directly and challenging their sense of the world and place in it. Of all pre-modern writing, except Shakespeare's, the *Canterbury Tales* seems most likely to confront students in this direct way. The intellectual pleasures and profits involved in a Chaucer course are inextricably entwined—you can't learn from Chaucer's work without having fun, and you can't have fun without exploring the complexities of Chaucer's representation of felt life in late medieval England.

The course I am describing here is a semester-long seminar open to advanced undergraduates and graduate students, and limited to about fifteen registrants. Most recently it included an equal number of undergraduates and graduates, but I should add that our undergraduates are no strangers to literary theory (having taken a required course called Interpretive Practices) and can hold their own in class discussions. We read nearly all the *Canterbury Tales* first, and then *Troilus and Criseyde*. All of us meet together for three hours a week, and the graduates convene for a "fourth hour" during which we discuss extra readings, primarily in literary and cultural theory as it connects with Chaucer studies. This is, I realise, a rather unusual arrangement, but I hope that some of my strategies and the reasons for them will prove useful to teachers in other institutional settings. I think the goals of the course—to understand and enjoy Chaucer's two great poems and to develop interpretive insight into the language and culture of a past era—are widely shared.

I would like to begin by describing some of the hermeneutic thinking I have found useful in reading Chaucer for fun and profit and then turn to specific classroom techniques that put these historical and aesthetic ideas into practice. Raymond Williams's work is a helpful starting point in locating the historical implications of Chaucer's work, especially in his discussions of "structures of feeling" and "dominant, residual and emergent" forms of social discourse (Williams 1977: 121–35). The value of Williams-esque underpinnings for a Chaucer course is that "history" need not be taken as a stable monolith against which ideas and images must be measured, but a multiple, porous, open-to-interpretation account of the experience of past generations. This approach to historical study aims to clarify for ourselves the issues that made Chaucer's work so important for its first audiences. To justify our pleasure in the *Tales* as art, I call on Immanuel Kant's position on disinterestedness and imaginative freedom from a final end (the famous "purposiveness without a purpose"). To show how historical and aesthetic attention can be invoked simultaneously, I turn to Hans-Georg Gadamer's hermeneutics. These three lurk about all semester, sometimes directly, but more often implicitly, inflecting the vocabulary with which we address the *Tales*.

The classroom practices I have found useful for this hermeneutic involve close attention to "keywords" (another aspect of Williams's influence) and a requirement that each student research and represent the point of view of one of the pilgrims in discussions from time to time. Both of these strategies flow from Gadamer's leading ideas: that "being that can be understood is language" (Gadamer 2003: 306) and that "historical alienation is mediated" by a "fusion of horizons" (2003: 374) by which he means regaining "the concepts of a historical past in such a way that they also include our own comprehension of them" (2003: 389). Gadamer allows a way to explore Chaucer's relation to the larger medieval culture while at the same time validating our current readings: a work of art speaks to different ages in different ways, yet retains "the trace of its original function" (2003: 120).

Theory: Williams's historicism, Kant's aesthetics, Gadamer's hermeneutics

Although everyone who studies older works *has* an implicit theory of history, most of the time we expect students to work out for themselves how the social context of a previous era elucidates and/or constrains fiction. The expectation with which students enter a course like "Chaucer" usually involves some version of one of these ideas: 1) that social history is a progress narrative in which each new development brings us closer to our current enlightened state, 2) that our ancestors were just like us, though differently dressed, sartorially and linguistically, or 3) that the differences between Chaucer's world and ours is so great that his texts require translation and gratify a mainly antiquarian interest. Although they can't all be invoked simultaneously, each of these three attitudes contains a partial truth.

In favour of the progress narrative, there is, of course, the importance of historical causality, the dependence of one event on another. On the other hand, it cannot account for the wise aspects of past social formations that lay inert for centuries, some perhaps lost to contemporary thought, nor for spikes of renewed vitality for residual ideas. And "progress" assumes an attained plateau of civilisation or quality of life today that is itself a contested issue. Williams helps us see an earlier world in which some of our own folkways are emerging—for example, suspicions of lawyerly sophistication (*General Prologue*, lines 309–30)— while some dominant medieval commonplaces seem archaic or hard to get one's mind around at all.

The second point—universalism under the unfamiliar surface—accords with the immediacy of some of our responses to Chaucer's humour or pathos, but it can misidentify those Chaucerian effects rendered hard to read by linguistic or social changes over time. Some such changes reach so deeply into the ways authors regard their characters that we need historical perspective to probe their underlying significance. For example, the various sumptuary laws regulating dress (probably unsuccessfully) suggest that clothing was expected to bear social meaning, allowing Chaucer a range of descriptive effects that *we* need historical inquiry to appreciate. This, in turn, affords Chaucer rich possibilities for specificity, but also irony and ambiguity: is the Prioress's fastidiousness a feature of her respect for the dignity of her calling or a social pretension that unmasks her desire for courtly graces? The implications of Chaucer's semantic choices for the narrator, the pilgrims, and their characters may be similarly analysed as both structured by an overarching cultural formation and driven by specific traits and desires—they are both structured and intimately personal, even for fictional persons. Williams's assertion that "no generation speaks quite the same language as its predecessors" (1977: 131) saves us from the fruitless argument that forces us to choose between calling the pilgrims allegories of their estates or regarding them as entirely individual in our own terms. On this issue we can have our cake (historical specificity) and eat it too (contemporary relevance).

The third preconception—the one that focuses on alterity and historical distance—is too stern about the nonetheless important insight that one's historical location has a good deal to do with what can be intuited in the first place and expressed as public discourse, that is, about historical situatedness. Here Williams asserts helpfully that "no dominant culture ever in reality includes all human practice, human energy, and human intention" (1977: 125). The questions "did medieval people really believe X?" or "could anyone have felt Y as early as this?" must always be answered provisionally. Some ideas may be genuinely unthinkable in a particular era, but all one can say with certainty is that the historical record does or does not retain evidence of them. Interpretation only a generation ago often too firmly excluded emergent structures of feeling on the grounds of an overwhelming dominant— I can remember when it was a simple matter to define the Wife of Bath as a laughably grotesque sinner and Margery Kempe as a hysterical madwoman. Now we are free to entertain the prospect that not everyone was a born-again Boethian—including Boethius. This enhanced sense of imaginative freedom—for medieval writers and for our reading of them—is clear in Williams and not unrelated to Kant.

Although Williams himself is not averse to aesthetic appreciation or analysis, most of his followers until very recently have been.[1] Two of Kant's positions in particular have come under attack: that apprehending beauty is a disinterested act and that the coherence and imaginative force exerted by beauty seem driven by purpose but do not finally conform to any conceptual purpose ("purposiveness without purpose"). These premises are taken to mean that Kant's kind of "disinterested and *free* delight" (Kant 1952: 49) is incompatible with a serious concern with social realities and social justice. I consider this a mis-reading of the *Critique of Judgement*, which argues that calling something beautiful is alleging that it pleases even though no concept can be found to accurately represent it. The appeal of beauty is not that it gives us what we want ("interest" in Kant's sense) or that its value can be proved conceptually (which is the appeal of the good).

Art that "quickens" both imagination and understanding without conforming to any one rational concept is judged beautiful, but that judgment cannot be proved, only called attention to. Moral precepts, of course, can be subjected to conceptual logic, and often they are involved in art as well, especially in narrative art. Kant's point, though, is that calling a work "beautiful" is different than calling it "good," though any particular beautiful object may be "understood and reduced to concepts" as a separate matter (Kant 1952: 117). One may, therefore, appreciate something aesthetically from which one does not expect benefits, even moral benefits: that is disinterestedness. I was recently in this position with regard to a chocolate fountain in a hotel in Las Vegas, Nevada—I disapproved of its wastefulness and showiness, but was none-the-less awed by the ingenuity of its design, its graceful trajectory, and its exquisite colours. The beautiful, then, eludes defining concepts and personal interests; it sometimes takes us by surprise, before we can assess its "correctness," as in the case of the cascading chocolate.

Much of the pleasure we have in reading Chaucer arises from just this state of affairs. We would not approve of a modern Griselda's self-effacing submissiveness if it were discovered by a social worker making a home visit, but various formal elements in the Clerk's telling of the tale keep us fascinated until the puzzling balance between cool allegory (Griselda as soul obedient to God) and domestic tragicomedy (Griselda as wife ultimately exonerated) is achieved in Part Six. Neither concept will adequately account for the tale, yet it haunts understanding; it is tightly coherent (purposive) in making use of all its details—without arriving at a final purpose. Once having experienced this disinterested coherence, we can go on to condemn Walter, his subjects, and medieval gender politics (as we should), but the story's hold on imagination may have established itself on account of its intricate formal beauty.[2]

Neither the historicism of Williams's concern with the social nature of art nor Kantian aesthetics is sufficient in itself, I think, to provide a theoretical foundation for the study of Chaucer. Even together, although not directly contradictory, these two vantage points can pull interpretation in different directions. It is Gadamer's position in *Truth and Method* and "Aesthetics and Hermeneutics" (from *Philosophical Hermeneutics*) that can explain how the *Canterbury Tales* kindles imagination with both direct aesthetic pleasures and the pleasure of informed historical insight.[3] Although narrative art appears to be addressed immediately to its reader, it none the less requires hermeneutic attention to quicken the words of a long-dead author. This is, of course, of special importance for Chaucer because the six-hundred-year gap between his language and social reference and ours is so large. It is a way of bringing the universalism of what I have designated the second likely student preconception (Chaucer's people are just like us) together with the situatedness of the third (aren't they interesting in their weirdness). Gadamer posits a "fusion of horizons" to explain how it is that we can reach a valid understanding of a text from the distant past, without claiming it to be identical with its fourteenth-century reception.

The student who enters class with a heightened sense of situatedness is aware of an important aspect of historical study: that there are limits to what can be imaged in a particular era. Gadamer calls this a "horizon of understanding," and that somewhat metaphoric phrasing has useful implications. Horizons seem more expansive than the ideological constraints of "situations" less bounded by social custom, more open to imaginative reach, and more amenable to change as one moves around. Horizons *do imply constraints, though*, on both the author's side and the reader's. Understanding a fiction must be sought even though its author creates it within certain boundaries and the reader recreates it within others. Gadamer's solution is not the attempt to regain through study an exact replica of the author's horizon. The very nature of language dictates that art *necessarily* means more than the author could have consciously intended. He therefore argues that the reader should acknowledge his own fore-conceptions (prejudices) and be willing to modify or abandon them as the narrative continues. The author's horizon is not an inert, fully objectified, construct, but involved in an unfolding conversation with the reader, whose vantage point is also amenable to change. The conversation can only take place because of the remarkable properties of language, properties that allow Stephen Greenblatt to pursue his wish to "speak with the dead."[4]

When Gadamer insists that "being that can be understood is language" (1976: 31) he implies that historical insight emerges through language, the magic thread that hermeneutics follows back toward the world of a long-dead predecessor like Chaucer. The realities and constraints of that world, happen within, not "behind the back" of language (1976: 35). Greenblatt would agree, calling language the "greatest collective creation" a culture produces (1995: 230), and it is precisely that collective, social aspect of linguistic creation that builds the bridge across time required for a fusion of horizons. In Gadamer's words, to fuse horizons is to "regain the concepts of a historical past in such a way that they also include our own comprehension of them" (2003: 374). It goes without saying that no single course could fuse our horizons (and of course modern horizons are not identical either) with the whole range of Chaucer's—the work must proceed in terms of details: in my case, specific words and character's social roles.

Playing the word game

This great cultural creation *language* must be widely understood publicly, yet available for an infinite number of particular, idiosyncratic instantiations. Chaucer's English (along with Wyclif's, but that is another story) was particularly influential in both establishing a broadly understood London dialect much enriched by semantic borrowing and in demonstrating the capacity of English to accommodate those subtle effects that enable literary sophistication. That's another thing students should know about Chaucer. The word game that operates throughout the seminar brings together the social reference held in word histories (a glance back to Williams) with the art of Chaucer's verbal wit (the play-fulness alluded to by Kant): paronomasia, stylistic parody, deliberate ambiguity—*Amor vincit omnia*. This game is a classroom practice that informs discussion of each of the tales, but also an exercise, different for each student, that serves as the germ of an assigned essay.

Here is how it works. Throughout the seminar, we devote class discussion time to inquiry into particular words that turn up repeatedly, like *privetee*, *gloss*, and *aventure*. At first I make a point of the word's range of meanings in Middle English, and use this range to point to interpretive cruces, like the *Amor* on the Prioress's amulet. The Wife's three instances of *gloss* each make a slightly different point (two refer to biblical exegesis, the third to the bedroom), but explaining their import for Chaucer's first audiences requires commentary on the Lollard position on glossing, and when we encounter the Summoner's three instances, a sustained opposition to glossing begins to appear as a shadowy implication across the text. The value of this approach to Gadamer's hermeneutic programme of "clarifying and mediating by our effort of interpretation what is said by persons we encounter in tradition" lies in its specificity. I have always had trouble figuring out how to present a firm picture of the late Middle Ages without totalising and thereby distorting the context of the literary texts; this sustained emphasis on words presents society and culture in their complexity and takes up strands of both continuity and change in the language. It is an admittedly partial way of getting at historical issues, but as instances accumulate through the semester, a rich mosaic begins to appear.

Another part of the word game involves a prepared paper. Each student focuses on a word or word pair that caught his or her attention, researches its medieval history (*OED* and/or *MED* and the Chaucer *Concordance*), and charts its relevance to one or two of the tales. In a recent course, for example, a student selected "brotelnesse" and "sikernesse," as the keywords in January's decision to marry (*Merchant's Tale*), showing how they participate in the irony that the "siker" bliss and rectitude he seeks become "restrictive, claustrophobic" "brotelness" within his own marriage. Another student concentrated on "magyk" in the *Franklin's Tale*, tracing it from the "tregetour's" trick with the rock to the proposition that the real magic in the tale was the mutuality of Arveragus and Dorigen's vows, which removed the rocks of "maistrie" that had dominated the marriage debate. Commentary on virginity and wifehood developed for another student into an answer to Howard Bloch's "Chaucer's Maiden's Head: The *Physician's Tale* and the Poetics of Virginity."[5]

The language game brings together the social import of Chaucer's semantic choices with the playful (not reducible to a stable concept) coherence of the *Tales* as art. My hope is that it also opens out into a hermeneutic practice useful for understanding other eras and other authors—a literary theory that accommodates historical study. And as Augustine pointed out in Book XI of *Confessions*, the present is so fleeting that most of what we can think about is history.

Performing social roles

The second feature of this approach asks each student to choose a pilgrim through whose eyes to try to see and ultimately judge the tale-telling. Once we have read the *General Prologue*, each student selects one pilgrim to research and adopt as a medieval vantage point from which to read the tales. In discussing some tales, I ask the students to represent the vantage point of "their" pilgrims. This exercise demands a vigorous, sustained call upon each student's historical imagination, which is, of course, being continually informed by the word game. To get students started on their research, I make suggestions to each "pilgrim" for reading relevant documents and general accounts from Abelard's *Historia calamitatum* for the Clerk to Boccaccio on plague for the Physician, and sections of Owst's *Literature and the Pulpit in Medieval England* for the Parson.

Because more reading is done to follow up on these initial hints, each student finds him or herself in the position of being an "expert" on some facet of medieval life, making the discussion of the tales genuinely informative for the rest of the class. These forays into medieval social practices and attitudes do not result in a required paper; instead they inform class discussions and contribute to the focus with which the second paper on the *Canterbury Tales* is handled. This aspect of the course also mimics the divisions in reception that I think probably characterised Chaucer's medieval audiences (a judgement, like Williams's, that no dominant discourse completely saturates all thinking in a period).

Sometimes these enacted identifications with the social locations of the various pilgrims results in imagining whole personalities, raising "hot" questions like: does Chaucer present us with individualised characterisations instead of "types," and would medieval discursive horizons have allowed him to do so? The students understand the prevalence of typological tendencies in the Middle Ages, but when they try to imagine themselves as listeners to each others' tales, they do not seem able to be entirely defined by "their" estates. For example, the "Pardoner" found himself admiring the *Nun's Priest's Tale* for cleverly manoeuvring a beast fable into a comic exemplum about pride, while he privately identified with the sly fox.[6] The "Prioress" publicly censured the *Wife's Prologue* as "too coarse," but admitted that she secretly enjoyed the clever way Alisoun managed to exercise power. The "Miller" (no proto-feminist) was impressed by Walter's trickery in the *Clerk's Tale*. The "Wife of Bath" justified her own tale as her "brilliant dream of happiness." And the "Franklin" opined that the Squire in his story is the "most fre" because he was not in the end "overcome by his own desires" but overcame them to become *fre* in the sense "noble." The "Monk" was indignant because the concluding scene of the *Nun's Priest's Tale* seems a parody of a hunting party (and therefore a jibe at him) and the barnyard frame too respectful of poverty; his response is coloured by jealousy of the Priest who succeeds in pleasing where he had failed.[7] The responsibility for attempting to see through the eyes of a particular medieval characterisation has produced results like these in many of my Chaucer classes; it has drawn me to the side of the scholarly controversy that stresses individuality over typology.

The uses of published commentary

All the students are required to sample a rich array of critical commentary on Chaucer and his era in writing their second paper on the *Canterbury Tales*. Although recent critical work has both proposed new insights into the period and suggested new angles of vision from which to see the *Tales*, I also stress the usefulness of older critical positions, since the history of criticism is not *necessarily* progressing toward some sort of stable perfection (any more than history itself is). The pedagogical value of sampling critical work on one's pilgrim and tale comes from coping with different interpretations of Chaucer's words. This second paper asks students to demonstrate their grasp of the *logic* of a sampling of published criticism and their independence in extending and/or disputing its conclusions for their own arguments.

The graduate students' papers are yet more complicated in that they are asked to appeal explicitly to some aspect of literary theory we have discussed in their "fourth hour" meetings. These reading vary from year to year; this is the list from the most recent course (specifics for these appear in "Works Cited"):

On "time": Augustine *Confessions*, Book XI and excerpts from Mary Carruthers's *The Book of Memory*
On hermeneutics: excerpts from Hans Robert Jauss's *Question and Answer*
On modern philosophical implications: Mark Miller's "Naturalism and Its Discontents"
On feminism: Mary Carruthers's "The Wife of Bath and the Painting of Lions"
On comedy: excerpts from Henri Bergson's *Laughter*, Northrop Frye's *Anatomy of Criticism*, and Freud's *Jokes and the Unconscious*
On deconstruction: H. Marshall Leicester's "Structure as Deconstruction"
On alchemy: Peggy Knapp's "The Work of Alchemy"
On allegory: Northrop Frye, *Anatomy of Criticism* and Fletcher's *Allegory*
On biblical allusion: Lee Patterson's "The Subject of Confession"
On irony and allegory: Larry Scanlon's "The Authority of Fable"
On misogyny: excerpts from D. W. Robertson's *Preface to Chaucer* and Carolyn Dinshaw's *Chaucer's Sexual Poetics*

These discussions are aimed at showing young scholars how literary theory can be interpreted and put to work for Chaucerian critical commentary. The critical essays use theory in various ways both to see the *Canterbury Tales* freshly and to structure an argument. In the short run, these extra readings give the graduate students models for their term papers and contribute ideas for the rest of the class discussions of the *Tales*. In the longer run, they help prepare them to write conference papers and publishable studies of their own (which some of them have done).

Festivity

All this looks like sustained and difficult intellectual work, and it is. But it is also infused with the pleasure of discovery and the more immediate aesthetic pleasure provided by Chaucerian narrative and verbal artistry. The last meeting of the discussion of *Canterbury Tales* features a festive symposium (both debate and eating, as a symposium was for the Greeks), to survey the tale telling and select the winner of the contest, whose student counterpart becomes the guest of honour at a modest lunchtime feast. Actually, there are two debates and two votes, one for their pilgrims' judgements, one for the students' own. Voting as "their pilgrims," the recent contest proved a three-way tie between the Knight, Merchant, and Nun's Priest, but no two voters for the same tale gave the same rationale. The winner from a modern point of view was the Franklin, whom several students praised for posing a problem close to their hearts: how can seizing one's own freedom be reconciled with granting others theirs.

This symposium demonstrates the way the historical progress narrative, universalism, and appreciation of alterity (the three attitudes most students enter the course with, see above) have been combined and deepened during the semester. Lively controversies about the ethical tenets of a tale or its shapeliness suggest that the Gadamerian perspective mandating a fusion of Chaucerian and current horizons has paid off. What I have seen in these discussions is precisely the overcoming of historical alienation, as everybody enters into the construct "late English Middle Ages" we have developed together, all the time knowing that it was constructed with modern discursive fore-conceptions. The variousness of the conclusions expressed in the class has prevented the hardening of this participation in Chaucer's world with the familiar "what Chaucer is trying to teach us" formulations that sometimes pop up when long-loved art is studied. In spite of its hold on imagination, the *Canterbury Tales* slips away from the concept or precept that would constrain its comic or philosophic play. And in the course, we still have *Troilus and Criseyde* to consider.

Notes

1. They have seen Williams as more deeply involved in ideology critique than his own words indicate, words that reject both single-minded attention to ideology and the overvaluation of formal beauty:

   If we are asked to believe that all literature is "ideology," in the crude sense that its dominant intention (and then our only response) is the communication or imposition of "social" or "political" meanings and values, we can only, in the end, turn away. If we are asked to believe that all literature is "aesthetic" in the crude sense that its dominant intention (and then our only response) is the beauty of language or form, we may stay a little longer but will in the end turn away. (Williams 1977: 155)

2. I have suggested a sequence moving from aesthetic apprehension to ethical judgement, but of course the order might be reversed. Even more likely is that the two kinds of apprehension are developed in tandem.
3. In "Aesthetics and Hermeneutics" Gadamer begins by acknowledging the immediacy of art, pretty much in Kantian terms:

    For of all things that confront us in nature and history, it is the work of art that speaks to us most directly. It possesses a mysterious intimacy that grips our entire being, as if there were no distance at all and every encounter with it were an encounter with ourselves . . . Only in a limited way does it retain its historical origin in itself . . . the aesthetic consciousness can appeal to the fact that the work of art communicates itself. (Gadamer 1976: 95–6)

4. The first sentence of *Shakespearean Negotiations* is "I began with the desire to speak with the dead."
5. Denizens of the New Chaucer Society will remember Bloch's paper from the 1988 meetings. The students whose work is reported in this paragraph are, respectively Elizabeth Hoiem, Eve Chen, and Rebecca May, the respondent to Bloch.
6. This insight, which read both the *Nun's Priest's Tale* and the characterisation of the Pardoner fits Leicester's estimate of the Pardoner as a self-conscious critic of orthodox pulpit practice—the link to published criticism is discussed below.
7. The students are, respectively, Kevin Bulter, Diana Laczny, Michele Cronin, Gretchen Underwood, Annalisa Schaefer, and Amanda Hamlin.

Works cited

Abelard, Peter. *The Story of Abelard's Adversities*, trans. J. T. Muckle. Toronto: Pontifical Institute of Medieval Studies, 1964

Augustine. *Confessions*, trans. John K. Ryan. Garden City, New York: Doubleday, 1960

Bergson, Henri (1912). *Laughter: An Essay on the Meaning of the Comic*, trans. Cloudesley Brereston and Fred Rothwell. New York: Macmillan

Bloch, Howard (Fall 1989). "Chaucer's Maiden's Head: *The Physician's Tale* and the Poetics of Virginity", *Representations*, 28: 113–34

Carruthers, Mary (1979). "The Wife of Bath and the Painting of Lions", *Publications of the Modern Language Association of America*, 94: 209–22

———. (1990). *The Book of Memory: A Study of Memory in Medieval Culture*. Cambridge: Cambridge University Press

Dinshaw, Carolyn (1989). *Chaucer's Sexual Poetics*. Madison: University of Wisconsin Press

Ellis, Steve, ed. (1998). *Chaucer: The Canterbury Tales*. London and New York: Longman

Fletcher, Angus (1964). *Allegory: The Theory of a Symbolic Mode*. Ithaca: Cornell University Press

Freud, Sigmund (1960). *Jokes and their Relation to the Unconscious*, Standard Edition, vol. 8 (1905), trans. James Strachey. London: Hogarth Press

Frye, Northrop (1957). *Anatomy of Criticism, Four Essays*. Princeton: Princeton University Press

Gadamer, Hans-Georg (1976). *Philosophical Hermeneutics*, trans. and ed. David E. Linge. Berkeley: University of California Press. The essay was originally published in 1964

———. (2003). *Truth and Method*, 2nd revsd edn, trans. Joel Weinsheimer and Donald Marshall. New York and London: Continuum Books

Greenblatt, Stephen (1988). *Shakespearean Negotiations*. Berkeley and Los Angeles: University of California

———. (1995). "Culture", in *Terms for Literary Study*, ed. Frank Lentricchia & Thomas McLaughlin. Chicago: Chicago University Press

Jauss, Hans Robert (1989). *Question and Answer: Forms of Dialogic Understanding*, trans. and ed. Michael Hays. Minneapolis: University of Minnesota Press

Kant, Emmanuel (1952). *Critique of Judgement*, trans. James Creed Meredith. Oxford: Clarendon Press

Knapp, Peggy A. (Fall 2000). "The Work of Alchemy", *Journal of Medieval and Early Modern Studies*, 30: 575–99

Leicester, H. Marshall (1998). "Structure as Deconstruction", in *Chaucer: The Canterbury Tales*, ed. Ellis. London and New York: Longman: pp. 23–41

Middle English Dictionary (1952–2001). Ann Arbor: University of Michigan Press

Miller, Mark (2000). "Naturalism and its Discontents", *English Literary History*, 67: 1–44

Oizumi, Akio (1991). *A Complete Concordance to the Works of Geoffrey Chaucer*. Amsterdam: Hildesheim

Owst, G. R. (1933). *Literature and the Pulpit in Medieval England*. Cambridge: Cambridge University Press

Oxford English Dictionary (1989) 2nd edn. Oxford: Oxford University Press

Patterson, Lee (1998). "The Subject of Confession: The Pardoner and the Rhetoric of Penance", in *Chaucer: The Canterbury Tales*, ed. Ellis. London and New York: Longman: pp. 169–88

Robertson Jr, D. W. (1962). *A Preface to Chaucer*. Princeton, NJ: Princeton University Press

Scanlon, Larry (1989). "The Authority of Fable: Allegory and Irony in the *Nun's Priest's Tale*", *Exemplaria*, 1: 43–68

Williams, Raymond (1977). *Marxism and Literature*. Oxford: Oxford University Press

2

A Series of Linked Assignments for the Undergraduate Course on Chaucer's *Canterbury Tales*

Steven F. Kruger

Teaching the undergraduate *Canterbury Tales* course at Queens College of the City University of New York (CUNY) presents particular challenges—in part related to its complex position within the Queens curriculum, in part the result of the College's situation as a large urban commuter campus serving an extraordinarily diverse group of students. The county of Queens is one of the most ethnically diverse in the United States (Malone et al. 2003: 9) and the student population of Queens College—often immigrants and the children of immigrants, many of whom speak English as a second language—reflects this diversity.[1] In addition, while Queens has a significant group of students who are of traditional college age, a large portion of the student body transfers from two-year colleges, and many students return to school after (sometimes lengthy) hiatuses in their education.[2]

While Queens is, within the CUNY system, noted for its strength in the liberal arts, and while English is a popular major at the College,[3] students (even prospective English majors) arrive at Queens with widely varying levels and kinds of literacy. Students who show themselves, in class discussions, to be intelligent and insightful may struggle in writing formal essays, and their research skills are often limited to the most superficial use of on-line or library resources. The situation in the Chaucer classroom is complicated by the fact that the *Canterbury Tales* fulfils several roles within the curriculum. While it is an upper-level course that English majors may take as an elective, it also fulfils two requirements within the College's "general education" scheme—the "pre-industrial or non-Western civilization" requirement and the "Tier II" humanities requirement (before registering for a "Tier II" course, students have completed an introductory course in the humanities, but this might be the only university-level humanities work they have done other than a required one-semester, first-year composition course). The lure of fulfilling two requirements with a single course means that many non-majors, even after they find out that the *Canterbury Tales* will be a demanding course, insist on registering for it.

In teaching Chaucer at Queens, then, one must address a variety of audiences: mature students with much experience of the world alongside nineteen-year-olds; those with lifelong experience speaking English alongside others who have learned English only recently; majors deeply immersed in English, American, and Anglophone literatures and cultures— some of whom are struggling to get by in the major, others of whom go on to graduate work in top-rank Ph.D. programmes—alongside students with little experience of reading complex literary texts hoping to get two general education requirements quickly out of the way.

Of course, the *Canterbury Tales* itself has much to say to all of these audiences, and one of my central goals in teaching the class is to introduce students as fully as possible to Chaucer's text, its complexities, its importance in an extended literary tradition, and the ways in which it might speak to twenty-first-century concerns at the same time that it addresses questions foreign to our place and time. While the series of writing assignments I present below can be adapted, I think, to most English classes that foreground both historical and critical material in relation to the literary or cultural text, there are many things that make a course in the *Canterbury Tales* unusual, even unique. Among the most striking of these is the way in which the course focuses on a *single* poetic work that is at one and the same time "unitary," fragmentary, and multiple. The rhythm of a semester's work on the *Canterbury Tales* differs significantly from that of a course focused on a series of discrete poems, films, plays, or novels (even ones related to each other through a single author or around a common theme). A reading of this simultaneously singular and multiple text builds across the whole of the semester; an accumulative interpretation of the text and its movements becomes central to the classroom discussion, sustaining an extended, increasingly nuanced, consideration of how the *Canterbury Tales* as a framed collection repeatedly takes up questions—about gender and sexuality, religious belief, and social organisation, for instance—from a variety of standpoints. In facilitating this accumulative work, I try to include all of the *Canterbury Tales* in the course syllabus, believing that, uninteresting to modern readers though some of the tales may usually be, *not* to read, say, the *Melibee* or *Monk's Tale* means to miss something important in the larger architectonics of Chaucer's text.[4]

The classroom discussions, involving, as they always do, a richly diverse group of students, are lively, contentious, engaged, and surprising—as when a modern orthodox Jewish student argues, in defence of Chaucer and his Prioress, that their anti-Semitism is not their own but determined by social assumptions that they cannot escape, or when a middle-aged married woman recognises in Walter's testing of Griselda something not so unlike her own expectations of the marriage relation. In my experience, however, the lively voices of the classroom tend to flatten out or falter in written assignments, and students who are good at expressing their responses to character, plot, and theme are less effective at analysing a text's nuances, and even less practiced at putting that text into historical or critical and theoretical contexts. To build work on research and writing more integrally into the course syllabus, I have moved from asking students, as I once did, to produce three or four "formal" essays across the semester to having them complete a series of briefer, more "informal" assignments that build to a single, concluding, "formal" essay. Each of the earlier assignments has students focus on particular kinds of work—close reading, historical research, responding to published critical essays—that need ultimately to be brought together and synthesised in the final essay. Working incrementally, the assignments are designed especially to guide students from outside the humanities in the kinds of complex thinking and writing that a critical essay informed by history entails (see Coles 1970 and Auten 2003 on the use of sequenced assignments in teaching writing; see Bard 1986 and Keating 1991 for interesting uses of such assignments in other contexts). I hope that, in moving through the series of assignments, students get a hands-on sense of how scholars working in the humanities pose and think questions through, marshal evidence, and construct arguments. The work students do in writing, as well as the in-class discussion, introduces them to different ways of thinking critically than would be emphasised in the natural science classroom (with its attention to experimental method) or the social science classroom (with its work in interpreting quantitative and qualitative material). I also believe that this kind of sequential assignment is useful for those already practiced in writing critical prose. In the English major at Queens, writing assignments most often ask for close reading, without research, either critical or historical, being an integral part of the work; many accomplished English majors experience significant difficulty incorporating other critical voices into their own writing and connecting texts in significant ways to historical contexts. The writing for the *Canterbury Tales* course asks students to do both these things. Breaking down into component parts the kind of work that goes into a critically- and historically-informed interpretive essay, the assignments help even the most skilful writers see, and get further intensive experience with, the set of processes that go into writing such an essay. In sum, I want all students in the class—whether majors or non-majors—to come away from the course more practiced writers and more confident and canny researchers. The assignments outlined below make no attempt to ensure "coverage" of the Chaucerian text, instead asking students to focus on a relatively small section of the *Canterbury Tales* (often, just one or two tales); they become "expert" in this small portion of the text (even as they are involved in reading and discussing the whole of the *Canterbury Tales* in class) through being immersed in work that I hope will carry over into other academic endeavours.

The series of assignments that structures the written work in my *Canterbury Tales* course includes four "low-stakes" or "informal" assignments (which I call "projects/critical responses"); these build to a final, "formal," fifteen-page essay, which must incorporate both published critical voices and historical research. The assignments are sequenced as follows (in the outline below, I note the main objectives for each of the individual assignments):

Project/Critical Response #1: translation of Middle English (attention to language, linguistic difference and change); close reading (attention to linguistic and poetic detail, literary effect, text and larger poetic context)

Project/Critical Response #2: posing and addressing a historical question pertinent to reading the *Canterbury Tales* (attention to the text and its contexts; historical research; planning to incorporate historical material into a reading of part of the *Canterbury Tales*)

Project/Critical Response #3 and Group Work: further exploring historical questions in relation to the Chaucerian text (pursuing a more extended programme of research; beginning to develop topic areas and theses for the final essay); responding to others' ideas and research strategies in small groups (with the hope that students' response to others' work will make for more self-critical approaches to their own projects)

Project/Critical Response #4: working with published critical material (attention to research; reading, understanding, summarising, and responding to critical discourse; developing interpretive ideas in relation to others' arguments)

Final Essay: incorporating historical and critical material into a strongly
argued interpretive essay.

Language, poetics, close reading

We work with the text of the *Canterbury Tales* in the original Middle
English, and so it is imperative, early in the course, to focus a significant
amount of attention on language and reading. I want students to grapple with the difficulties of Middle English for several reasons. Students,
especially less experienced readers, tend to focus all of their attention on
plot, character, and theme. Of course, all of these are important in a
course on the *Canterbury Tales*, but if the course is also to be about *poetry*,
it needs to pay close attention to language, and for Chaucer this means
the 'original' Middle English. To use a translated text is, to my mind, to
capitulate to the idea that the *Canterbury Tales* can be effectively discussed just as a collection of stories, with intriguing characters, taking
up a set of controversial themes; I am not ready—despite the additional
difficulty of teaching the text in Middle English—to make that capitula-
tion. In addition, the students' struggle with this other, older version of
English allows for an engagement with significant questions about language and linguistic change: What is the relation of fourteenth-century
English to the subsequent incarnations of the language? How does
English, in the present moment of "world Englishes," continue to
change? What, indeed, constitutes English? Such questions are invari-
ably of interest to students (whether native or non-native speakers)
whose own version of English is in everyday life often called into question, even denigrated. In working with Middle English, we do much in-
class reading aloud and translation, especially toward the beginning of
the semester; there are also unannounced translation quizzes throughout the semester. And the first written assignment for the course, done
after we have read and discussed the *General Prologue* and the *Knight's
Tale*, focuses to a significant degree on language.

This first assignment begins by asking students to choose a brief
passage from a section of the *Canterbury Tales* they have already read and
to translate that passage into idiomatic Modern English. I mark the
translations carefully—providing in my written comments corrections
but also alternative readings; I do this in order to suggest that the "correct"
translation is often something we could debate, itself subject to interpretive choices. As a second element of the first assignment, I ask students
to comment on their own translations, noting especially linguistic difficulties they encountered in translating. Often students are effective at

identifying the difficulties they have had in working with a passage; but often, too, they find it hard to pinpoint the larger, sentence-level and syntactical, difficulties of the text, instead focusing their comments on individual difficult words. Responding to this section of the assignment provides an opportunity for directing students who may have translated effectively word-for-word but without recognising the overall syntactical structure of the passage back to the difficulties of Chaucerian (and Middle English and poetic) syntax.

While students grapple with Chaucer's Middle English, they also, as part of this first assignment, work on developing the practices of close and critical reading with which they have already engaged in courses prerequisite to mine. I ask students to focus on at least one poetic or literary effect that they find striking in the passage they have translated and to comment on *how* this operates. And I ask students to reflect more generally on the significance of the passage they have been working with. The commentary here of course often connects back to classroom discussion; the assignment gives students an opportunity to test in writing the kinds of interpretive stances we have begun considering as a class and to stake out positions of their own within the multivoiced debate of the classroom.

In responding to this first assignment, I pay close attention to details of language and poetic effect—modelling back in my written response the kind of careful and reflective attention to detail that the assignment asks students to demonstrate. I often point out ways in which students might push their own observations—for example, on metre or rhyme—further, or additional Chaucerian passages in which the use of a device like metaphor operates differently from the one they have chosen to comment on. And in response to their remarks on a passage's significance, I raise questions that would lead them to develop their thinking further or, alternatively, to consider a different sort of reading than the one they have developed. Such detailed written comments of course take a significant amount of time to compose, but I believe that they pay off—not only in getting students to think more fully about the material taken on for this assignment but also in setting them on the route toward more careful, fuller, and more thoughtful engagement with Middle English and with the *Canterbury Tales* throughout the semester. I emphasise in this assignment that students are not expected to produce a "formal" essay, and that they can take on the discrete tasks and questions posed piecemeal. But I also assign a grade for this piece of writing, as for all the subsequent "informal" or "low-stakes" writing involved in the course (see Elbow 2002 on the assessment of "low-" and "high-stakes" writing). Assigning grades and having the projects count toward the final course grade emphasises that these are required and serious components of the coursework (see Greenberg 1998; Yancey 1999; White 2001 on assessment more generally).

Researching historical contexts, reading historically

I am concerned, in all my undergraduate medieval courses, to have students consider the relations between a text and its historical contexts. This is an important part of the class discussion, where we talk about Chaucer's life, official duties, and social status; the place of poetry and the poet in Ricardian England; late-medieval social, political, and religious institutions, and changes occurring in these. But I also want students actively to engage in historical research and to reflect on how such research might change their reading of a literary text or cultural object. Such work tends to be particularly difficult for students when literary works inhabit historical moments, like the medieval, that are distant—both chronologically and in terms of their cultural assumptions and understandings. The next two writing assignments are intended to lead students into confronting such historical difference and to help them gain some experience in doing historically grounded research. (Project/Critical Response #2 is due in the sixth week of a fourteen-week semester; the work of Project/Critical Response #3 then stretches through the seventh, eighth, ninth, and tenth weeks.)

In the first of these two assignments, I ask students to pose a historical question whose answer they think might be useful for the reading of Chaucer's poetry. By this point in the semester, we have already asked a significant number of such questions in class—thinking, for instance, with the *Man of Law's Tale* about the relations among Christianity, Islam, and Judaism; late-medieval Christianity's memory of its pre-Christian past; the uses of 'Old Testament' texts in Christianity's self-conception; Mediterranean trade routes and England's implication in these; Chaucer's possible knowledge about the "exotic" places evoked in the tale; the historical interimplication of (royal) conversion and marriage; secular women's piety; and so on. In addition, as part of the assignment itself, I offer examples of different kinds of historical question that might be posed. I emphasise that students can raise any kind of historical question, as long as it truly interests them and has real potential for illuminating some aspect of Chaucer's *Canterbury Tales*.

In the work they hand in, students are asked first to articulate the question they have posed and then to suggest *why* and *how* they feel that addressing this particular question would be illuminating for reading Chaucer. They then report on research they have done in response to their question. I have asked them to find at least two sources—one of which must not be an Internet site—that provide useful information. They then summarise what they have learned from these sources. Often students find and comment on more than two sources, but working with two provides a good starting point. Most students' first impulse is to surf the Web for material: sometimes, in doing so, they find useful sources, but more often not. The second, non-Internet source is often a book from the college library. Though the Queens library collection is not particularly distinguished or up-to-date in medieval materials, most of what students find is reputable and scholarly. Having the two sources in play in the assignment allows me, in my response to this assignment, to contrast the two, to ask which seems to be the most useful, detailed, and reliable; it thus allows for a discussion of how to assess a particular source's value.

With this assignment, I provide general guidance about the process of doing research. I explain why the Internet will not necessarily turn up the most interesting or helpful material. We discuss the difference between websites and full-text databases like JSTOR or Project Muse, and I give some hints about using those databases available through the college library. We also discuss why more recent sources will be most useful, especially early in the process of doing research (not least because these will provide further bibliographic leads, but also because they will tend to raise the scholarly questions currently eliciting the strongest interest).

As part of the written assignment, after students have described and summarised the sources they have found, they reflect briefly on how they would further pursue their research. This provides a way for them to recognise that this first assignment is not an end in itself but instead the first step in a more extended course of research that leads to the final essay. My comments on this assignment also emphasise the assignment's initiatory nature, trying to point students toward ways of narrowing and sharpening their historical questions, and of thinking through more fully how the answers to their questions might change their readings of the *Canterbury Tales*. If a student says simply that s/he is interested in investigating "religion" in the *Canterbury Tales*, I ask him/her (first) to focus on a particular tale and (second) to specify what about "religion" seems important for a reading of that text. If the student chooses to work on the *Prioress's Tale*, for instance, we consider together whether it is the relationship between medieval Christianity and Judaism that calls for further understanding, or the nature of late-medieval English female religious communities, or the history of Marian devotion (and so on). I also provide explicit suggestions for further research: if students have not yet examined article databases, I recommend that they look at these; if students have not yet looked at the physical resources available in the library—especially books—I point them in that direction. Again, as with the first assignment, I assign a grade to this work: I assess how effective students have been in posing specific and useful historical questions; how thoughtfully they have articulated the ways in which their question might reflect on a reading of the *Canterbury Tales*; whether they have found pertinent and scholarly sources, and whether their summaries of those sources give a good sense of the material they contain; and how effectively students articulate a future programme of research.

Throughout the semester, I am concerned with having students con-front questions about academic honesty and plagiarism, but this second assignment—where, for the first time, students are asked in their written work to engage with others' writing—makes such questions especially pertinent. In giving the assignment, I am careful to foreground the dis-tinction between summary and *verbatim* quotation, to note how any direct quotation must be indicated in the student's text, and to focus on how sources should be cited. The English Department at Queens has an official statement on plagiarism, and I distribute this at the start of the semester, discuss it then, and return to it when students receive the assignment for Project/Critical Response #2. At this point in the course, I also have students do an exercise on the proper citation of sources; tak-ing a page of critical prose and stripping it of its footnotes, I ask students to identify all the places where the author—whether citing verbatim or summarising someone else's ideas—would need to include a note. Despite all this work, however, students do sometimes present, instead of summaries, verbatim quotation unmarked by quotation marks; I hold conferences with students who do so, hoping to head off future trouble with plagiarism.

It is in this part of the course that I have students engage in small group work. I divide the class into three- or four-person groups based on the research topics they began to pursue in the second writing assign-ment. This allows students working on similar kinds of material to pool their research findings and to respond to each other's approaches: this helps them rethink or expand their historical investigation. One student working on religious history and the *Prioress's Tale* might be looking at everyday religious practices while another might be exploring official Church doctrine. In responding actively to others' ideas and research, students will (I hope) also come to think more critically about their own. At this point in the course, students also begin formulating ideas for their final essay, which builds on the research work they have so far accomplished. Here, the groups provide a useful social space within which students approaching similar topics can "brainstorm" together. Much of the scholarly literature on small group work focuses either on its role in second language acquisition or on its place in the composition classroom. In the latter context, group work often is tied closely to the process of revision. I use group work in the *Canterbury Tales* class, however, at the point when students are generating ideas for their essays. Ideally, group interactions would take place throughout the essay writing process, with students responding both when ideas for the paper are being generated and when a rough draft of the paper has been submitted. Making time for this additional step in the series of assignments laid out here, however, would mean having to rethink the timing of the whole series—and probably some of the earlier work would need to be eliminated (see Jones 1989; Squint 2002; and Folsom 2004 for scholarship about the place of small groups in the literature classroom). It's also the case that, while students may be writing on the same tale and asking similar historical questions, they have begun to arrive at very different conclusions. Such differences are useful to highlight—as the group work does—as students refine and develop their ideas.

While I compose the groups mostly around topics of interest, I also try to distribute the students so that those who have done the best written work are *not* all placed together. Mixed groups provide "weaker" students especially useful feedback. It might seem that the "stronger" students lose out in such an exchange, but in practice those who may not be as careful readers or as practiced writers often are able to pose effective questions about their peers' work (just as, often, their voices in classroom discussion are insightful). And "stronger" members of the groups gain something useful for their own work in having the opportunity to help others improve the quality of their work (see Rubino 2004 for one discussion of the effective teaching of "mixed ability groups," in a very different context).

The group work lasts four weeks. In week one, students exchange copies of Project/Critical Response #2 and begin discussing the historical questions they have posed, the possible relations of these to readings of Chaucer, and the historical research they have done. In week two, students bring in, for each other member of their group, a brief commentary on their peers' Projects/Critical Responses #2 in which they (1) note both strengths and weaknesses, (2) raise questions about the other group members' research work to date, and (3) make suggestions about where this work might next go, including how it might form the basis for a final essay on Chaucer. At this point, students also prepare, distribute, and discuss a brief Essay Proposal, in which they sketch initial ideas for their final essays (attending especially to how these might grow out of their historical research). During week three, students prepare, for each other member of their group, responses to these Essay Proposals. I ask that the responses (1) comment on both strengths and weaknesses, (2) make suggestions for how the paper topic might be further developed and/or narrowed, (3) propose further research that might be useful in the writing of the essay, and (4) raise questions about the paper topic that might help in its development. Finally, during week four, students hand in Project/Critical Response #3, which consists of (1) the Essay Proposal, revised after considering peer responses, (2) copies of students' responses to their peers' Projects/Critical Responses #2, (3) copies of students' responses to their peers' Essay Proposals, and (4) an update on progress toward the final essay. In the last part of this assignment, I ask students to assess how the comments received from other members of their group have been helpful, to summarise any additional research they have undertaken, and to comment on ways in which their ideas are developing for the final essay.

In responding to this assignment, I try to add my voice to the peer responses, without my comments taking over as authoritative. I am therefore more laconic than in responding to earlier assignments, and I often largely reiterate (and sometimes clarify) suggestions made by peers. I also, of course, sometimes have different kinds of suggestions to make, and, in highlighting how these might lead down a different road than would the peer comments, I want students to recognise not that my response is better but that, in considering the various responses, they, as authors, have certain interpretive decisions to make. I know that I have done my job well when students take the advice of their peers in directions that are productive for the final essays.

I do assign grades for Project/Critical Response #3, and these are individual grades rather than grades given to the groups as a whole. Group grading here seems inappropriate, since—while students work together—they are individually responsible for each writing task. In assessing students' success with this assignment, I attend not only to the student's development of her/his own research and ideas but also to the ways in which s/he has engaged with fellow students' work. I reward students for being attentive and helpful to others, believing that such attentiveness benefits not only those receiving feedback but also those providing it, helping to show them new ways of thinking about their own work.

Finding and reading criticism

I also want students to become familiar with current critical approaches to Chaucer. Though this is particularly important for English majors, and especially those bound for graduate programmes, non-majors also learn something significant about work in the humanities by engaging with recent scholarly and critical writing. We discuss critical approaches and arguments in class (I include a few recent essays about the *Canterbury Tales* on the course syllabus as well as some theoretical extracts not directly related to Chaucer or the Middle Ages; for reflection on how queer theory might be used to organise a course on Chaucer, see Burger and Kruger 2003). But I also want students to be able to find pertinent published work on their own, and to read that work with understanding. Project/Critical Response #4 is addressed to this goal. In my experience, students will most easily find books, and certainly Internet sources, on Chaucer, so, in this assignment, I focus on having them locate recent articles. In working with published criticism, students often find themselves grappling with a kind of prose that they find difficult, so I ask them to summarise the argument of one critical essay. And many students have trouble incorporating others' voices into their own writing, quoting sections from a critical article without making clear how these help the development of their own argument. Project/Critical Response #4 allows students, before they come to the final essay, to reflect on how a published essay might contribute to their own thinking. (This assignment is generally due in the eleventh week of the semester; students begin it while they are still finishing Project/ Critical Response #3.)

This assignment—like the historical research done for Projects/Critical Responses #2 and 3—is directly tied to the final essay for the course, which asks students to develop their own reading of one or two of the *Canterbury Tales* while engaging with both historical material and published critical interpretations of the *Canterbury Tales*. Students focus their work for this assignment on one of the tales they have already identified as central to their final essays. I ask them to find a recent critical essay about that tale in one of the following journals: *Chaucer Review, JEGP, Philological Quarterly, Speculum, Studies in Philology,* or *Studies in the Age of Chaucer.* The research required here is thus, for several reasons, more directed than that I have had students engage in earlier. First, and most pragmatically, all of these journals are fully available in the Queens College library. Further, I want students to use a journal that is not posted on the Internet; many students remain attached to surfing the Web for material, and I ask them instead to use the resources of the college library—whether in hard copy, on microfilm, or through full-text databases. I also want to be able to discuss with the class what characterises scholarly journals, like all of those listed here, as well as what differentiates journals from each other (*Speculum*, with its more historical bent; *JEGP*, *PQ*, and *SP*, with their continuing attachment to an idea of "philology" and their wide-ranging contents; and *ChauR* and *SAC*, with their much narrower focus on questions Chaucerian).

The assignment asks students to search for pertinent articles using the MLA Bibliography, and it includes a guide to using the MLA. I ask students to find as much material as possible pertinent to the topic they have begun to develop for the final essay, but then—for the purposes of this assignment—they focus on a single article, which they are to read carefully. They hand in (1) a summary of the article, in which they are to identify clearly its thesis and its main arguments, (2) a list of points from the article that they have found particularly useful and interesting, (3) a list of points about which they have questions or with which they disagree, and (4) a paragraph in which they indicate how they would develop their own reading of Chaucer's tale in response to the essay studied.

In responding to and grading the assignment, I attend to how successful students have been in following directions, navigating the MLA bibliography, and using the library's resources. I assess whether the essay they have found is pertinent to the project in which they are engaged (if not, I provide further suggestions about how to find such material). And I assess and comment on their facility in reading, understanding, and posing questions about difficult, technical, scholarly-critical writing.

The work of synthesis

Finally, I want students to be able to bring together their close engagement with Chaucer's language and text, their historical research, and their reading of other critics' work into an interpretive essay with a strong thesis and argument. I think students are more likely to reach this final goal if—as in this class—they have a series of explicit assignments leading up to the final essay. In my course, work for the final essay actually begins quite early on, and, as a result, students tend to be less overwhelmed than by the prospect of writing an ambitious final essay *ex nihilo*. They also, in small groups, have had the opportunity to formulate essay topics in conversation with several classmates as well as the instructor. This facilitates the identification of a topic and thesis that will be able to sustain the more extended argument required by the final assignment.

In the assignment for the final essay, I remind students that they are to develop their own topic, focusing attention on one or two tales (or sections) of the *Canterbury Tales*. I emphasise that the essay should develop a strong interpretive thesis and argument about whatever particular question they pose. I also remind them that the historical research they have done and the critical material they have found needs to be incorporated into the final essay. I ask them to return to their previous assignments and to think through how the work they have already done supports and strengthens their interpretations of the Chaucerian text.

The final essay is "high-stakes" and "formal," rather than "low-stakes," "informal," writing. Some students, of course, fail effectively to bring together all the elements required by the assignment—historical context, scholarly criticism, and their own interpretations and arguments. But many do succeed, producing more historically and critically informed work than in previous versions of the course where I did not approach the final essay through the sequenced assignments described here. One recent student, for instance, read the *Clerk's Tale* through Wyclif's political writings and alongside critical assessments of Chaucer's relation to "Lollardy" (this won an English Department prize). Another did extensive research on Jewish–Christian relations and used this, along with critical work like Fradenburg's on the *Prioress's Tale*, to arrive at a thoughtful reading of that tale's representation of Jews. Most students succeed at least in thinking historically about the *Canterbury Tales*, and in beginning to engage with complex critical writing.

For those students who don't do particularly distinguished work on the final essay, but who have worked hard throughout the semester, the fact that the projects/critical responses are graded is a relief. While the final essay is still the part of the course that is weighted most heavily (there is also an in-class final examination, which makes students responsible for the whole of the *Canterbury Tales*), excellent work on the projects/critical responses can mean that a student receiving a C for the final essay might still earn a B for the course.[5]

I think that it would be possible to adapt this series of assignments to a course in which the final essay and examination were the only graded components. But, even here, I would recommend that the work done on the earlier projects/critical responses be considered in assigning a grade to the final essay—and that it be made clear to students, from the start, that their "low-stakes" writing becomes part of a portfolio of work leading up to the final essay and assessed, alongside it, at the end of the term. Again, only if students take seriously the earlier assignments will these effectively guide them toward the final essay itself.

Notes

1. See Queens College, at
   http://qcpages.qc.cuny.edu/Institutional_Research/ FACTBOOK/
   ethnicU.html, and
   http://qcpages.qc.cuny.edu/Institutional_ Research/FACTBOOK/
   2004Country.html.
2. See Queens College, at
   http://qcpages.qc.cuny.edu/Institutional_Research/ FACTBOOK/
   transferStudents.html, and
   http://qcpages.qc.cuny.edu/ Institutional_Research/FACTBOOK/
   ageUnderg04.html.
3. See Queens College, at
   http://qcpages.qc.cuny.edu/Institutional_Research/FACTBOOK/
   uMajorsSpr04.html.
4. The history of Chaucer criticism also shows tales once thought "uninteresting" often being (re)discovered as of particular interest. See, for instance, the treatment of the *Tale of Melibee* in Burger 2003 and of the *Monk's Tale* in Fradenburg 2002.
5. Each of the projects/critical responses counts for 8% of the final grade, while the final essay counts for 30%: the aggregate grade for the four projects/critical responses thus neatly balances the final essay grade. In addition, the final examination counts 25%, in-class participation 8%, and language quizzes 5%.

Works cited

Auten, Janet Gebhart (2003). "Helping Students Decode the Difficult Text: 'The Yellow Wall-Paper' and the Sequential Response", in *The Pedagogical Wallpaper: Teaching Charlotte Perkins Gilman's "The Yellow Wall-Paper"*, ed. Jeffrey Andrew Weinstock. New York: Peter Lang: pp. 130–43

Bard, Imre (1986). "Sequencing the Writing of Essays in Pre-Modern World History Courses", *History Teacher*, 19: 361–71

Brown, Peter, ed. (2002). *A Companion to Chaucer*. Oxford: Blackwell

Burger, Glenn (2003). *Chaucer's Queer Nation*. Minneapolis and London: University of Minnesota Press

———. & Steven F. Kruger (2003). "Queer Chaucer in the Classroom", in *Teaching Literature: A Companion*, ed. Tanya Agothocleous & Ann C. Dean. Basingstoke: Palgrave Macmillan: pp. 31–40

Coles Jr, W. E. (1970). "The Sense of Nonsense as a Design for Sequential Writing Assignments", *College Composition and Communication*, 21: 27–34

Elbow, Peter (2002). "High Stakes and Low Stakes in Assigning and Responding to Writing", in *Dialogue on Writing: Rethinking ESL, Basic Writing, and First-Year Composition*, ed. Geraldine DeLuca, Len Fox, Mark-Ameen Johnson, & Myra Kogen. Mahwah, NJ: Erlbaum: pp. 289–98

Folsom, Marcia McClintock (2004). " 'I Wish We Had a Donkey': Small-Group Work and Writing Assignments for *Emma*", in *Approaches to Teaching Austen's Emma*, ed. Marcia McClintock Folsom. New York: Modern Language Association: pp. 159–68

Fradenburg, L. O. Aranye (2002). *Sacrifice Your Love: Psychoanalysis, Historicism, Chaucer*. Minneapolis and London: University of Minnesota Press

Fradenburg, Louise O. (1989). "Criticism, Anti-Semitism and the *Prioress's Tale*", *Exemplaria*, 1: 69–115

Greenberg, Karen L. (1998). "Review: Grading, Evaluating, Assessing: Power and Politics in College Composition", *College Composition and Communication*, 49: 275–84

Jones, Rowena Revis (1989). "Group Work as an Approach to Teaching Dickinson", in *Approaches to Teaching Dickinson's Poetry*, ed. Robin Riley Fast & Christine Mack Gordon. New York: Modern Language Association: pp. 62–9

Keating, Barbara (1991). "Using Staged Assignments as Student Spotters: Learning Research Methods", *Teaching Sociology*, 19: 514–17

Malone, Nolan, Kaari F. Baluja, Joseph M. Costanzo, & Cynthia J. Davis (December 2003). "The Foreign Born Population: 2000", *U.S. Census Bureau*: http://www.census.gov/prod/2003pubs/c2kbr-34.pdf

Queens College. Office of Institutional Research. Factbook http://qcpages. qc.cuny.edu/Institutional_Research/factbook03.html

Rubino, Antonia (2004). "Teaching Mixed-Ability Groups at Tertiary Level: The Case of Italian", *FULGOR: Flinders University Languages Group Online Review*, 2: 22–42: http://ehlt.flinders.edu.au/deptlang/fulgor/volume2i1/papers/fulgor_ v2i1_rubino.pdf

Squint, Kirstin L. (2002). "Non-Graded Group Work and Role-Playing: Empowering Students toward Critical Analysis", *Eureka Studies in Teaching Short Fiction*, 2: 103–6

White, Edward M. (2001). "The Opening of the Modern Era of Writing Assessment: A Narrative", *College English*, 63: 306–20

Yancey, Kathleen Blake (1999). "Looking Back as We Look Forward: Historicizing Writing Assessment", *College Composition and Communication*, 50: 483–503

3

Why We Should Teach—and Our Students Perform—*The Legend of Good Women*

Fiona Tolhurst

At the 2004 meeting of The New Chaucer Society in Glasgow, the panel discussion of how to teach the *General Prologue* inspired me to want to continue the pedagogical dialogue.[1] Hoping to stimulate discussion of the Chaucerian canon and non-traditional pedagogies, I proposed a session on teaching *The Legend of Good Women* for the 2006 Congress. The organisers rejected that proposal due to scheduling pressures, but it is likely that they could not risk offering a session about a poem few Chaucer scholars value. Nevertheless, to encourage my colleagues to rethink both their syllabi and pedagogies, I will argue that students, teachers, and the field of Medieval Studies will all benefit if we teach *The Legend of Good Women* and our students perform it.

The Legend of Good Women as an integral part of the syllabus

Because my first medieval literature course did not include Chaucer and my first Chaucer course covered all but a few of his works, I neither view nor present *The Canterbury Tales* as the poet's greatest or only master-work. Consequently, my goal as a Chaucer instructor is to facilitate the process of students' developing their *own* assessments of his works. This goal is consistent with the characteristics of high-quality instruction: "quality of explanation and stimulation of student interest," "concern and respect for students and student learning," "appropriate assessment and feedback," "clear goals and intellectual challenge," students' "independence, control, and active engagement," and the instructor's learning from students (Ramsden 1992: 96–103). To facilitate students' developing their own analyses, I require them to read all texts in Middle English in the Riverside edition (although students may consult a translation to aid comprehension, for example, Cowen & Kane 1995; for a helpful discussion of how to use a translation as a "shoehorn" into Middle English, see Remley 1996; for a more detailed discussion of the costs and benefits of teaching Chaucer in translation, see Sinclair 1954). This requirement challenges students to interpret Chaucer's language for themselves rather than read a translation that must—since it is an interpretation—limit the range of their analyses. Because I want students to be my partners in constructing the meaning of Chaucer's Middle English, I, like L. M. Findlay, encourage specialist and generalist study that is both introductory and advanced, focused and scattered, entails a double gesture towards the canon, both revering it and roughing it up (Findlay 1999: 72). If my students choose to label *The Canterbury Tales* a masterwork, I want them to do so because they judge it to be the best of several works they have read—not because they know nothing else.

Although projects based on Chaucer's most famous work can produce active learning and the formation of a learning community, they reinforce academic values I wish to combat. Jean E. Jost in "Teaching *The Canterbury Tales:* The Process and The Product" documents a creative project in a major authors course that facilitated both active learning and the formation of a learning community (2000: 61–9). Her project required students to work collaboratively to create their own tale-tellers and to write tales for them in Chaucerian style, thus making it possible for undergraduates to imitate Chaucer as literary master while applying their knowledge of Middle English and the fourteenth century (2000: 62–3). However, the core values undergirding most Chaucer and major authors courses are ones I try to counteract through both the breadth of my syllabus and its acting component. One such value is that the Chaucerian text most "worthy" of study is *The Canterbury Tales*—a value most Chaucer and major authors instructors reinforce through their teaching of the *Tales* either to the exclusion of other Chaucerian works or as the grand finale to a Chaucer course. Another is that if students work with a great author's masterpiece, they can safely ignore the rest of his (and it usually is *his*) literary production. A syllabus giving students the freedom to judge a "great author" by his body of work, and to distinguish among those works, is one way to move beyond the "value this literature because I tell you it is great and spend time on it" model of teaching literature.

The syllabus and pedagogy in my one-semester stand-alone Chaucer course reflect the philosophy that students are my partners in learning.

The syllabus includes course readings and assignments we select together on the first day of class, and it requires each student to present a critical perspective on Chaucer and participate in a performance. It therefore "put[s] students in the center of learning, using their experiences to mutually construct meaning" (Baxter Magolda & Buckley 1997, cited in Brown 2004: 145). By identifying my own critical biases as well as offering students access to both mainstream and outlying opinions about Chaucer's works, I encourage students to come to their own conclusions about the relative value of Chaucer's works rather than approach them as "major" or "minor." So that students can decide for themselves how to value Chaucer's varied works, *The Canterbury Tales* are our starting point, not our finale. Teaching only *The Canterbury Tales* tells students which of the poet's works matters, as does praising and spending the majority of class time on the *Tales* after moving rapidly through Chaucer's short poems and skipping *Troilus and Criseyde*, *The Legend of Good Women*, or both. My including *The Legend of Good Women* certainly distinguishes my undergraduate Chaucer syllabus from most other ones, just as my discussing how to teach *The Legend* distinguishes this article from most articles about teaching Chaucer.[2]

The portraits in the *General Prologue* give students the opportunity to become comfortable pronouncing and scanning Middle English verse as well as to learn how to discern the grammatical functions and possible meanings of words. To facilitate comparative analysis, we then discuss pairs of Canterbury tales: the *Miller's* and the *Reeve's Tales*, the *Clerk's* and the *Wife of Bath's Tales*, the *Franklin's* and the *Friar's Tales*, the *Prioress's* and the *Physician's Tales*, and the *Pardoner's* and the *Summoner's Tales*. Reading the *Retraction* highlights the challenge of identifying the poet's tone and reinforces our awareness of Chaucer's playful presentation of pivotal issues: the textual authority of his sources and works, the idea of literary reputation, and the construction of social hierarchies based on class and gender. Study of *The Canterbury Tales*, along with some of their analogues, gives us access to the canonical Chaucer so that we can continually revisit our ideas about who Chaucer is as a narrator and what he achieves as a writer. Like many of my colleagues, I give students access to Boccaccian analogues for *The Reeve's Tale* (*Decameron* 9.6) and *The Clerk's Tale* (10.10) found in Boccaccio's *Decameron*. I also present the Petrarchan analogue for *The Clerk's Tale* (Severs 1942; Bryan & Dempster 1941). My goal is to pay respectful attention to the work Chaucer scholars value the most while encouraging students to express their own perspectives on the meaning and relative value (literary, entertainment, and political) of Chaucer's works through two 3,000-word essays, two exams, and a performance.

The second half of the course begins with *The Parliament of Fowls*, giving us an opportunity to compare a brief work to a longer one while continuing to discuss Chaucer's interest in issues of narratorial authority and social hierarchy. That conversation continues when students read a prose summary of the Prologue to *The Legend of Good Women* so that we can devote class time to the legends themselves. With this focus, we avoid either privileging the Prologue to *The Legend of Good Women* over the legends—as some critics do[3]—or treating the poem as inferior to *The Canterbury Tales*, as both A. C. Baugh (1963) and Larry D. Benson (1987) do in their editions of Chaucer's works. Baugh introduces *The Legend of Good Women* by focusing almost exclusively on issues concerning the two versions of the Prologue. He then concludes his brief comparison of the poem with *The Canterbury Tales*, "And no one will regret his devoting the energies of his remaining years to this incomparably greater project [*The Canterbury Tales*]" (1963: 215). A summary of the mainly negative critical reputation of *The Legend of Good Women* appears in Larry D. Benson's introduction to the poem in *The Riverside Chaucer* (1987: 587–88). One benefit of reading these tales about famous females is that students can compare Chaucer's two tale collections. Another is that they can connect Chaucer's questioning of traditional gender roles with contemporary debates about how Western cultures define normative masculinity and femininity. Still another benefit is that students can look at "the construction of Woman" in the legends and the *Wife of Bath's Prologue*, leading them to consider the places of these female-centred texts within both the Chaucerian canon and the canon of English literature (Hahn 1992: 434). Furthermore, through student presentations of critical responses to Chaucer's works and group comparison of several tales from Giovanni Boccaccio's *Famous Women* [*De mulieribus claris*] with Chaucer's legends, students develop into Chaucer critics who come to appreciate Chaucer's method of translation and shifts in tone.

From *The Legend of Good Women* we move to *The House of Fame*, which playfully undermines Chaucer's authority as narrator and mocks the desire for literary fame. Then, while the performance groups are at work, each student generates a summary of part of Boccaccio's *Il Filostrato* before we read Chaucer's and Shakespeare's stories of Troilus and Criseyde. In this way, we discover "why it is accurate to suggest that Chaucer influenced the dramatists—most fundamentally Shakespeare—who came after him" (see Beidler 1996: 493; see Thompson [1978] for a full-length study of Chaucer's influence on Shakespeare and other Elizabethan and Jacobean dramatists; Donaldson argues that Shakespeare read Chaucer "with full appreciation of his complexity" [1985: 2]).

Although other teachers have used comparative analysis to encourage students to debate the significance of Chaucer's works (see, for example, Findlay 1999; Pinti 1996), pairing Chaucer's and Shakespeare's tales of Troilus and Criseyde requires students to reconsider key assumptions: where they draw the generic line between drama and narrative poetry, whether Shakespeare is "great" in light of his unsympathetic portrait of Criseyde, and whether renaissance literature is "better" than medieval. Studying two of English literature's biggest names can also lead to fruitful discussions of how a writer becomes a "major" author. Pinti (1996) offers an example of an undergraduate course that makes "the construction of the figure of a major author" a central concern; Trigg, however, questions the idea of a Chaucer course by questioning the assumption that Chaucer is a better writer than his contemporaries (2002: 349). The inclusiveness of my syllabus gives students the freedom to reach their own conclusions about which works they value and why. One such conclusion appeared in a student evaluation in the form of advice for me: "Maybe spend less time on *The Canterbury Tales* because the other stories were much more entertaining." As this comment suggests, teaching *The Legend of Good Women* in an inclusive course can turn students into Chaucer critics. Nevertheless, performing several legends allows students to apply their critical skills—educating both themselves and their instructor.

The Legend of Good Women in performance: the rationale

Although "the primary learning environment for undergraduate students, the fairly passive lecture-discussion format where faculty talk and most students listen, is contrary to almost every principle of optimal settings for student learning," most professors continue to use that format as their primary mode of teaching (Guskin 1994: 20). This pedagogical choice is part of what makes contemporary academic culture so out of step with the primarily oral and visual culture of today's university students (for further discussion of working with students operating primarily in an oral culture, see Folks 1996). Using this format also runs counter to Howard Gardner's theory of multiple intelligences that has caused many educators to vary their teaching methods, thus facilitating the academic success of students possessing various combinations of intelligences (1995: 77–99). Robert B. Barr and John Tagg, along with others who promote learner-centred teaching, define the undergraduate teacher's job as "creat[ing] environments and experiences that bring students to discover and construct knowledge for themselves, to make students members of communities of learners that make discoveries and solve problems" (1995: 15). One means of creating such an environment and facilitating the development of learning communities is a co-operative learning activity. In such an activity, "the group as a whole must complete some task together, but the information to be learned or skills to be acquired must be mastered by each individual in the group" (Starko 1995: 278). Students can learn about Chaucer through class discussion, but they are more likely to internalise their knowledge of how to pronounce Middle English and develop literary analyses if they apply it. Therefore, I ask students to explore a text as members of a learning community that develops its own interpretive agenda and offers them access to the joy of speaking Middle English aloud, bearing in mind Clare R. Kinney's question concerning how instructors can avoid "naturalizing certain ideologically inflected assumptions" (1996: 457).

I recognise that some of my colleagues assume an acting project is inherently less rigorous than a traditional paper or exam; nevertheless, in my experience, such a project is at least as rigorous as traditional methods of assessment. Since the degree of focus and amount of effort individual students devote to writing a paper or studying for an exam varies tremendously, student learning varies greatly. To complete a performance, however, every student must be at least reasonably well prepared if for no other reason than to avoid public embarrassment. A performance project, therefore, guarantees a minimum level of effort that ensures substantial learning. It also allows students to benefit from one another's strengths in a class in which both foreign language and English grammar competencies vary widely. Contemplative learners can contribute their textual analyses and gain confidence as performers, active learners can improve their understanding of a text as they shape a script, and learners with an ear for poetry can aid colleagues with pronunciation and metre. Evaluation of a non-traditional assignment often gives rise to faculty concerns about rigour, so the evaluation of this project included a discussion during which students explained their interpretive choices, as an exam or paper requires.

The project of performing *The Legend of Good Women* developed in a ten-student undergraduate seminar at Alfred University, a 2000-student comprehensive university, but it could work equally well for a larger class split into working groups of three to five people. On the first day of class, students voted to perform scenes from Chaucer's works rather than write a third 3,000-word essay. Although they used an acting studio for dress rehearsals and performances, any classroom with movable furniture or lecture hall with a podium area would serve just as well. A large class would require some booking of rehearsal spaces, but students could rehearse in private spaces if given several days off from regular class time. To keep costs low and creativity high, our productions used minimal props and costumes.

The goal of the acting project was to make the group's interpretation of the text visible to an audience. That interpretation might explore the tale's moral (or lack thereof) as well as its shifts in tone, presentation or revision of traditional gender roles, and blending of genres. The project's parameters put students into what Barr and Tagg have called "holistic, complex, meaningful environments organized around long-term goals"—groups through which they applied their knowledge of these interpretive issues (1995: 22). Success in this project, however, depended upon their complete artistic freedom: to edit texts for performance, develop staging and costuming, experiment with cross-gender casting, and use rehearsals to explore the moments at which Chaucer frustrates audience expectations and puts his characters in awkward, or even silly, situations. This freedom made it possible for students to demonstrate wisdom, the "capacity to internally construct an interpretation of events, drawing on available evidence to render judgments in circumstances with no easy answers" (Brown 2004: 143). The task of developing, without supervision, a textual interpretation and then performing it required group members to construct a shared understanding of the text and to make judgements about how to present that understanding—a circumstance in which there are no "easy answers."

The Legend of Good Women in performance: the process

Step 1: Planning

Several weeks before the performance date, students used a fifty-minute class meeting to form small groups based on shared interest in a Chaucerian text performable in ten to fifteen minutes and then to consider casting, staging, and editing issues. The groups were free to perform a brief work, a particular tale or legend, or a coherent segment from a longer work; however, all three groups quickly chose to perform tales from *The Legend of Good Women*: "The Legend of Thisbe," "The Legend of Lucrece," and "The Legend of Cleopatra." Their choices showed me how powerfully an instructor's selection of materials and manner of presenting them affect student perceptions of which literary works have value, but their explanations of those choices revealed how attractive *The Legend of Good Women* is to student performers for practical reasons. All three groups noted that the individual legends are brief enough to perform in ten to fifteen minutes, offer opportunities for various readings of the same lines, and are naturally dramatic because of the many suicidal lovers who inhabit them. By voting with their feet, my students demonstrated the dramatic potential of this work that many undergraduate syllabi omit. Furthermore, their choices suggest that *The Legend of Good Women* can be more accessible to undergraduates than *The Canterbury Tales* when students are freed from the burden of reading the *Legend*'s lengthy Prologue, extant in two significantly different versions (see *The Riverside Chaucer*, ed. Benson, 588–630, and *The Legend of Good Women*, ed. Cowen & Kane, 169–200 and 325–44). Peter G. Beidler has already championed the performance of students' short skits from *The Canterbury Tales* (Beidler 1996: 486–93) just as Lee Patterson has championed the performing and writing of students' fictional and musical responses to *The Canterbury Tales* (Patterson 1996: 518). Nevertheless, student performances of *The Legend of Good Women* can offer even greater educational benefits because of the multiplicity of readings each brief legend makes possible.

Step 2: Rehearsal

During three fifty-minute class periods, groups ran their own rehearsals in separate but adjacent spaces. Any group could schedule whatever additional rehearsals its members felt were necessary. I served as a consultant—answering questions about pronunciation, definitions of Middle English words, and the logistics of performance day. In Barr and Tagg's terms, I was the designer of "learning methods and environments," a supporter rather than a supervisor (1995: 17). I encouraged students to consider how gestures, facial expressions, and interactions with the audience and other characters could make the group's interpretation of the text visible; assured them that the bases of evaluation were textual interpretation and creativity of presentation, not acting talent; and reminded them that "bad" acting can highlight a text's meta-textual moments while creating comedy.

Step 3: Performance

With at least one actor in each production group doing intentionally bad acting, each text was taken to its comic and meta-textual limits. To provide a safe space for risk-taking on stage, the audience consisted of seminar members only. All three productions were engaging and reflected intense textual analysis, but each had its own dramatic flair.

The actor-directors of "The Legend of Thisbe" exploited the text's potential for absurdity because they felt the ending undercut the lovers' tragic deaths. They created comedy through the wall's narration of the love story and some spectacular cross-casting.[4] The narrator-wall spoke calmly but used her facial expressions to communicate her disdain for Thisbe and Pyramus. The man playing Thisbe spoke flawless Chaucerian English, but he made the audience crave the heroine's death by sounding like Miss Piggy on amphetamines. Like her acting partner, the petite woman playing Pyramus embraced gender-bending by behaving like ladies' man Tony Manero (John Travolta) in *Saturday Night Fever*. The contrast between the serene narrator and both the hysterical Thisbe and the less-than-sensitive Pyramus kept the audience laughing. Finally, Pyramus's sudden and silly death and Thisbe's frenetic one encouraged the audience to dismiss these fools.

The group performing "The Legend of Lucrece" interpreted this text as contrasting a clever and lusty Tarquinius with a dim and neurotic Lucrece. Therefore, after the actors created dramatic tension through underscoring Tarquinius's inappropriate sexual advances, they deflated it through the villain's cartoonish glee. The production stressed the legend's disconcerting shift from tragedy to bathos by having Lucrece first call on the narrator several times for her line while stumbling through her final speech, then cover her feet with her skirt out of neurotic fussiness right before she dies. Lucrece's whiny delivery and inability to die with style contrasted strongly with the rape scene, thus capturing the text's shift from tragedy to a mixture of bathos and comedy.

The actor-directors performing "The Legend of Cleopatra" exploited all the comic and meta-textual potential of their script. First, the narrator read from the textbook in his best Masterpiece Theatre voice and dress (complete with smoking jacket and pipe) until his sudden demise—like that of the Historian in *Monty Python and the Holy Grail*. Then, to portray the sea battle during which combatants slip on peas, two female sword-fighters parried on a slippery floor in high heels (ed. Benson, line 648). Next, the female actor playing Antony committed suicide after consulting the script (*The Riverside Chaucer*). Antony's shoulder shrug immediately before stabbing himself indicated his helplessness in the face of a narrative requiring his death. Finally, a male Cleopatra stood on a table while reciting her long pre-suicide speech. She then tried to tear off her toga and leap "naked" into the adder pit, but her wardrobe malfunctioned in a manner opposite to that of Janet Jackson's at the 2004 Superbowl—adding another layer to the audience's response. Both the cross-casting and the wardrobe malfunction highlighted how

Chaucer questions the roles of tragic heroine and hero in *The Legend of Good Women*. When Cleopatra removed the toga to reveal the "censored" tags covering her chest and private parts, the audience roared with laughter. She then leapt off the table to the floor where she rolled around with a four-foot toy snake at her throat. This sequence of actions stressed the dramatic nature of Cleopatra's suicide while exploring a quirk in the text—the nakedness of the heroine as she leaps to her death. This production, like the other two, made visible *The Legend of Good Women*'s many tone shifts and generic complexities.

Step 4: Evaluation

Putting the value of partnering with my students into action again, I facilitated a large-group discussion of all three performances immediately after their completion. During this session, actor-directors responded to the experience of acting in one piece and viewing two other pieces, and they asked questions about each group's interpretive choices. This debriefing served three key functions: it gave the actor-directors the freedom to use their own "judgment to determine the ultimate worth of a creative project" and thus add to their psychological safety (Starko 1995: 252); it gave me information about the students' creative process and their assessments of how developing and viewing performances affected their learning; and it allowed me to assess students' under-standing of the poem. Although one student later expressed a preference for an oral exam over a performance, her peers said during the debrief-ing that the performances were a positive experience (student evaluation form, April 2004). In the course of this discussion, students reported that performing, rather than just reading, Chaucer's *Legend* had required them to interpret the text actively—to edit it for performance, study it for sound and sense, and memorise verse. This work, they noted, had made their readings of Chaucer become more concrete and more nuanced. They also reported gaining confidence in their ability to speak Middle English aloud and enjoying the production process. Our discussion helped me to evaluate the productions, completed our discussion of *The Legend of Good Women*, and provided a high note on which to end the course.

Despite the positive effects of integrating creative projects into tradi-tional academic classes, I recognise that some college-level teachers resist including them either because they fear inflated grades or feel uncomfortable evaluating creative work. However, depending upon what part of the process she most wants to value, an instructor can vary the evaluation method. My method of assessment was to derive a score out of ten points (representing ten per cent of the student's final grade) based upon the quality of the production as well as the individual student's workload and creativity in the performance, facility with Middle English, and contributions to the large-group discussion session. I did not use a strict formula for this score, but an instructor could create a formula to weight these components as she sees fit; for example, production quality = 3 points, individual performance = 2, facility with Middle English = 2, quality of discussion = 3.

Another method of evaluation I have used for Shakespeare performances is that of student journals. In them actor-directors document their developing understanding of their own characters, their group's scene, and the play as a whole. Nevertheless, despite the additional basis for evaluation they provide, journals usually reward with a higher grade the more "academic" student—who tends to write with greater analytical depth and eloquence about the process—while punishing with a lower one any student with a "non-academic" set of intelligences. Therefore, whether an instructor includes a writing component in an acting project will depend upon what evaluation methods her department favours, and how traditionally academic she wants the acting project to be. Having students write a response paper after the performances serves an evaluative function similar to that of a journal, but again would favour the more "academic" students. Furthermore, adding any written component to an acting project can overload students: since developing a performance is at least as much work as writing a paper, the instructor must be careful not to kill people's enthusiasm for the project by splitting their energies. One component I will add next time, however, is a peer evaluation of the rehearsal process using a simple survey form. By asking each student to assess his or her own contribution as well as the contributions of other group members, I will receive data that will inform my evaluation of individual students without overburdening them.

The benefits of student performances for students

The educational and personal benefits of this project for both my students and for me were several and tangible, but they all stemmed from the healthy changes in our roles it required. For student-centred learning to happen, teachers must stop selling Chaucer and let students sell themselves on both him and the Middle Ages. By escaping the rigid structure of daily close reading in fifty-minute chunks, my students and I became colleagues who analysed Chaucer's verse more richly and creatively than we had before. This escape made possible the joy of co-operative work: the joy the students experienced as they discovered one of Chaucer's legends for themselves, and the joy they gave to one another and to me through their performances.

For my students, approaching *The Legend of Good Women* as a script had tangible educational benefits. Since they had to modify their roles in healthy ways, their performances made possible accomplishments that class discussion, lecture, and composing analytical papers did not. Academically strong students had to use their interpretive skills to benefit the group, rather than to get a high individual grade on a paper or exam, and take a chance they do not usually take: to play with material and risk appearing foolish. Students who had not routinely offered textual interpretations in class had to contribute to the group's analysis, developing their interpretive instincts in a supportive peer group. For those whose midterm exam results were less than solid, the project facilitated some stronger performances on the final exam: several students who gained self-confidence as actor-directors did significantly better on the final exam than they had done on the midterm exam.[5] These results are not surprising given that this project increased student engagement with the poetry, and "Depth of engagement is an important aspect of orientation to learning" (Brown 2004: 142). Projects requiring depth of engagement are essential if students are to be "equipped to face the challenges of adult life, characterized by changing conditions and a need for critical and independent thought" (Baxter Magolda 2002 and Kegan 1994, cited in Brown 2004: 142).

Meaningful connection with course material is the essential condition under which students can gain wisdom rather than knowledge: "Wisdom develops when students go through the core learning-from-life process, comprised of reflection, integration, and application" (Brown 2004: 137). This project helped students to acquire wisdom about both Chaucer and themselves by requiring them to live Chaucer's verse: they reflected on the processes of interpreting texts and pronouncing Middle English, integrated discoveries made during rehearsals with information learned during class discussions, and applied their knowledge to produce a visual and aural interpretation of Chaucer. One student, Albert Fassbender III, described how the project improved his awareness of Chaucer's comic touch, required students to design a Middle English script, and gave him a low-stress environment in which to work hard:

As for the experience of acting out the stories rather than taking a test or writing a paper on them, I think I found that the dramatic versions revealed much of the humor inherent in the texts, and furthermore proved an interesting exercise in Middle English composition since the texts had to be adapted to fit the stage, so to speak. Most importantly, however, I think they were just fun to do and to watch. I'm fairly certain that I put in far more work on the play than I would have on studying or reviewing for a test (although arguably less than I would have for a paper), wandering around, as I did, for several days before the performance, muttering to myself my lines in Middle English (which attracted not a few confused stares), putting in time planning and adapting the text, and taking trips to purchase needed supplies. There was, on the other hand, considerably less stress and worry to contend with as we were merely putting on an informal performance for our classmates and you, our professor. (E-mail, 15 September 2005)

In addition to the educational benefits of the project, there were tangible personal benefits for all ten students, with a couple of students making huge gains. In my roles as consultant and audience member, I had the opportunity to witness every seminar member become more confident in his or her skill in speaking Chaucerian English and saw two shy students, Pascale Anderson and Jon Hudack, make major gains. The senior female student who had always feared public speaking tremendously remarked recently, "after that, I'm pretty sure I could handle just about anything" (e-mail from Pascale Anderson, 1 February 2006). She also explained how the project helped her face her fear of public speaking:

I think my main concern wasn't so much getting the lines right or even pronouncing the words correctly. I just wanted to be able to actually speak. For me, it seems that no matter how much preparation I've had, my biggest obstacle is facing a room full of people and getting the words in my brain to somehow make it out of my mouth . . . I guess it was because everyone in the class seemed more focused on having fun with the work than getting it anywhere near perfect, I just took a deep breath and got on with it. And once I realised that people don't actually die of embarrassment (and, even if I were the first documented case, I don't think it would've mattered much to me for very long), things seemed to flow rather easily. (E-mail, 1 February 2006)

When I asked Pascale to comment on how the experience of acting impacted her, she revealed how my asking *all* students to speak Middle

English helped her to succeed:

> I think that the entire Chaucer experience made me feel part of the seminar group in that, I guess you could say, we were all speaking the same language. Especially in the beginning, when none of us students had ventured into the world of Middle English, I felt somewhat at ease knowing that each and every one of us was going to screw up a word or three . . . I think that, as the weeks went by, my confidence in the language grew, in that it wasn't so much of a chore as it once was. I found that I wasn't looking at the bottom of the page for definitions of the words I was reading as often as at the start of the term. I was retaining the meaning of some of the words and phrases that I had picked up from other passages! As for the presentation, I think it did help me connect with my peers. I think there was a sense of accomplishment, at least on my part, like we had done something. (E-mail, 2 February 2006)

Jon Hudack, a junior male student who had produced consistently strong written work but had tended not to volunteer comments during class, changed profoundly. He not only gained confidence within his peer group but also became a more outgoing student who now pursues his education with exuberance:

> Playing Cleopatra was an eye-opening experience for me. Not only did it help me develop an understanding of Chaucer's work, but it also helped me to be more comfortable as a student. The following semester, I was much more active and vocal in my English classes and as a resident assistant. I have taken on a lot more challenges in life since my opportunity to cross-dress and perform a scene in Middle English. Reading Middle English out loud caused me to feel more comfortable taking Spanish classes. I felt that, if I could pronounce "perced to the rote," I could say just about anything in Spanish and feel confident. Performing Chaucer wasn't the only confidence-booster I have received over the years, but every experience adds up. Now I am a DJ for the campus radio station as well as a lead news anchor for the campus television station. I'd say things have progressed quite a bit since my experience playing history's favorite drama queen. (E-mail from Jonathan R. Hudack, 18 November 2005)

These responses convince me that this acting project had a greater positive impact on my students than completing any paper or exam might have had.

Nevertheless, it would be dishonest not to acknowledge that speaking Middle English in public (even in a small, safe public of eleven people) is difficult. As my student Megan Shove demonstrates, however, those students who find performing Chaucer a formidable challenge benefit professionally and personally from rising to it:

> The idea of performing Chaucer was not that daunting to me; I was actually excited to be able to do something that combined my major (English) with what was then my minor (Theatre). Usually, acting is pretty easy for me; memorisation is always a snap, and projection and inflection come pretty naturally. With Chaucer, however, the Middle English threw me for a loop, and, somewhere along the line, all my usual confidence was lost. Come performance time, I found myself speaking quietly, afraid that mispronunciation would stand out like a sore thumb. I was concentrating so hard on the words themselves that I forgot to act, and even though I knew my lines, I found myself looking at the book, partially out of panic and partially for reassurance. Luckily, my confidence was lost only during the time I was on stage. The new and unexpected challenge of acting in what is practically a foreign language intrigued, rather than discouraged, me; here was an aspect of performance that went beyond any other form of acting I had ever done, and ever since I have wanted an opportunity to give it another shot, in hopes of improving upon my previous performance. This semester I jumped at the chance to take Medieval Drama, a course that incorporates performances of medieval texts in Middle English. I always love a challenge, and I feel more than ready to meet this one. (E-mail from Megan E. Shove, 24 January 2006)

Megan's self-awareness and growing mastery of performing in Middle English in our Medieval Drama course are powerful testaments to the educational and spiritual value of this project.

By completing a comprehensive course that includes *The Legend of Good Women* and transforming Chaucerian texts into performances, students can benefit from the joys and confidence-building of a creative group project and become Chaucer critics in their own right. Performances allow them to judge and interpret a text as they see fit and to set the critical agenda of the course along with their instructor. Asking them to write papers in which they feel pressured to agree with the teacher or prevailing critical opinion can stifle their development as thinkers and writers. In contrast, an acting project can empower students to write better exams and papers through forming a learning community in which every student gains confidence and competence. Freeing students to trust their own critical faculties, while supporting them as consultants, is the greatest gift teachers can give their students. Given the struggles many students have with writing traditional papers and exams, adding a performance component to a Chaucer course gives them the means to demonstrate their critical and linguistic skills and to become teachers as well as self-motivated learners.

Benefits for the instructor and Medieval Studies

The benefits my students gained through these performances made them well worth the half-dozen class periods necessary to develop them, but those same performances also provided me educational and personal benefits. *The Legend of Good Women* holds many interpretive possibilities for me now, thanks to my students. The next time I teach Chaucer, I will encourage my students to perform scenes from several works so that I can develop deeper understandings of those texts. Although the educational benefits were substantial, the personal ones were even more so: I became an ally and colleague of my students who is aware of how "professing" can stifle students' ideas. In addition, freed from my usual role of selling the Middle Ages, I had the pleasure of see-ing my students make Middle English a living language, the Middle Ages less remote, and a medieval text their own.

Furthermore, the project outlined here allows the teacher and students to form a learning community and thus avoid, or at least escape for several days, the top-down dynamic that traditional teaching methods create. While this dynamic can make medieval literature dead to our stu-dents, student performances make medieval literature and languages as alive to students as contemporary fiction. Therefore, more student per-formances of Chaucer could help Medieval Studies to thrive, rather than merely survive, in both the academy and popular culture. Performance projects are also one possible means of "defending the labour-intensive specificities of humanities teaching and scholarship" by getting students to perform that labour in a creative and enjoyable way (Findlay 1999: 72). Thomas A. Goodman has defined the "triple challenge" of medievalists: "to re-engage post-medieval colleagues of post-medieval sources as well as the sources themselves in our teaching, to invite new undergraduate and graduate students of the medieval, and to re-enter public discourse as crit-ical historians" (Goodman 1996: 471–2). If more medievalists make per-formances and other innovative methods centrepieces of our pedagogies, we will better engage our post-medieval colleagues with the languages and literatures we teach. Innovative pedagogies also invite students to engage the medieval period in ways relevant to them and encourage them to become "critical historians" who can assess popular versions of the Middle Ages and become "competent, capable, and interesting people" who will succeed at complex tasks in the world (Barr & Tagg 1995: 25). In addition, student performances send people into the world who have an appreciation for and understanding of Chaucer—people who might fight to keep Chaucer in university curricula. For both pedagogical and political reasons, then, we should teach—and have our students perform—Chaucer, especially *The Legend of Good Women*.

Notes

1. At the 15–19 July 2004 meeting of The New Chaucer Society, the panel "Re-reading and Re-thinking the General Prologue," organised by Jim Rhodes (University of Southern Connecticut), consisted of Howell Chickering (Amherst College), Rosalind Field (Royal Holloway University of London), Alan Gaylord (Dartmouth University), Anne Middleton (University of California Berkeley), Lee Patterson (Yale University), and R. N. Swanson (Birmingham University).
2. Even a thorough reading of Rose, ed. (1996), will give the reader little information about teaching *The Legend of Good Women* since only one of the ten contributors mentions it, and does so only in passing. Remley says he teaches "at least the Prologue and some representative portraits from the *Legend of Good Women*" (1996: 482). It is striking that Richmond's article outlines a syllabus she characterises as containing "wider reading" that omits *The Legend of Good Women* while including *Troilus and Criseyde*, early poems, and parts of *The Canterbury Tales* (1996: 501).
3. If one does a search in the MLA Bibliography for *The Legend of Good Women*, one can access about 200 articles out of which about 25 focus on the Prologue and the remainder offer little detailed coverage of any legendary female other than Dido. Perpetuating the treatment of the Prologue as separable from, and more worthy of critical attention than, the legends themselves is Robertson 2002.
4. It is noteworthy that my students did not make any conscious attempt to imitate Shakespeare's *Midsummer Night's Dream* although their production felt much like *Midsummer's* play within the play.
5. Students who scored 13.25, 15.35, and 12.3 out of 20 points on the midterm received a 17.3, a 16.9, and a 14.3 on the final exam, respectively.

Works cited

Barr, Robert B. & John Tagg (1995). "From Teaching to Learning—A New Paradigm for Undergraduate Education", *Change*, 27.6: 13–25
Baugh, A. C., ed. (1963). *Chaucer's Major Poetry*. Englewood Cliffs, NJ: Prentice-Hall

Baxter Magolda, Marcia B. (2002). *Making Their Own Way: Narratives for Transforming Higher Education to Promote Self-development*. Sterling, VA: Stylus
———. & Jennifer Buckley (March 1997). "Constructive-developmental Pedagogy: Linking Knowledge Construction and Students' Epistemological Development", Paper Presented at the Annual Meeting of the American Educational Research Association, Chicago, IL
Beidler, Peter (1996). "Teaching Chaucer as Drama: The Garden Scene in 'The Shipman's Tale' ", *Exemplaria*, 8.2: 485–93
Benson, Larry D., ed. (1987). *The Riverside Chaucer*. Oxford: Oxford University Press
Boccaccio, Giovanni. *The Decameron*, trans. G. H. McWilliam. Harmondsworth: Penguin, 1972
———. *Il Filostrato*, Italian text ed. Vincenzo Pernicone, trans. Robert P. ApRoberts & Anna Bruni Seldis. New York: Garland Publishing Inc., 1986
———. *Famous Women [De claris mulieribus]*, ed. and trans. Virginia Brown. Cambridge, MA and London: Harvard University Press, 2001
Brown, Scott C. (2004). "Learning Across the Campus: How College Facilitates the Development of Wisdom", *Journal of College Student Development*, 45: 134–48
Bryan, W. F. & Germaine Dempster, ed. (1941). *Chaucer: Sources and Analogues*, rpt New York: Humanities Press, 1958
Chaucer, Geoffrey (1987). *The Riverside Chaucer*, 3rd edn, ed. Larry D. Benson. Boston: Houghton Mifflin
———. (1995). *The Legend of Good Women*, ed. Janet Cowen & George Kane. East Lansing, MI: Colleagues Press
Donaldson, E. Talbot (1985). *The Swan at the Well: Shakespeare Reading Chaucer*. New Haven: Yale University Press
Findlay, L. M. (1999). "Reading and Teaching Troilus Otherwise: St Maure, Chaucer, and Henryson", *Florilegium*, 16: 61–75
Folks, Cathalin B. (1996). "Of Sundry Folk: The Canterbury Pilgrimage as Metaphor for Teaching Chaucer at the Community College", *Exemplaria* (Teaching Chaucer in the 90s), 8.2: 473–7
Gardner, Howard (1995). "The Theory of Multiple Intelligences", in *Multiple Intelligences: A Collection*, ed. Robin, Fogarty & James Bellanca. Arlington Heights, IL: IRI/Skylight Training and Publishing, Inc.
Goodman, Thomas (1996). "On Literacy", *Exemplaria* (Teaching Chaucer in the 90s), 8.2: 459–72
Guskin, Alan (1994). "Reducing Student Costs and Enhancing Student Learning: The University Challenge of the 1990s. Part II: Restructuring the Role of Faculty", *Change*, 26.5: 16–25
Hahn, Thomas (1992). "Teaching the Resistant Woman: The Wife of Bath and the Academy", *Exemplaria*, 4: 431–40
Jost, Jean E. (2000). "Teaching *The Canterbury Tales*: The Process and The Product", *Studies in Medieval and Renaissance Teaching*, 8: 61–9
Kegan, Robert (1994). *In Over Our Heads: The Mental Demands of Modern Life*. Cambridge, MA: Harvard University Press
Kinney, Clare R. (1996). "Theory and Pedagogy", *Exemplaria* (Teaching Chaucer in the 90s), 8.2: 455–7
Monty Python and the Holy Grail. dir. Terry Gilliam & Terry Jones. Python (Monty) Pictures, 1975

Patterson, Lee (1996). "The Disenchanted Classroom", *Exemplaria* (Teaching Chaucer in the 90s), 8.2: 513–45

Pinti, Daniel J. (1996). "Teaching Chaucer through the Fifteenth Century", *Exemplaria* (Teaching Chaucer in the 90s), 8.2: 507–11

Ramsden, Paul (1992). *Learning to Teach in Higher Education*. London and New York: Routledge

Remley, Paul (1996). "Questions of Subjectivity and Ideology in the Production of an Electronic Text of the *Canterbury Tales*", *Exemplaria* (Teaching Chaucer in the 90s), 8.2: 479–84

Richmond, Velma Bourgeois (1996). "Teaching Chaucer in a Small Catholic Liberal Arts College", *Exemplaria* (Teaching Chaucer in the 90s), 8.2: 495–505

Robertson, Kellie (2002). "Laboring in the God of Love's Garden: Chaucer's Prologue to *The Legend of Good Women*", *Studies in the Age of Chaucer*, 24: 115–47

Rose, Christine, ed. (1996). *Teaching Chaucer in the 90s: A Symposium, Exemplaria*, 8.2

Saturday Night Fever, dir. John Badham. Paramount Pictures, 1977

Severs, J. Burke (1942). *The Literary Relationships of Chaucer's Clerk's Tale*, Yale Studies in English 96. New Haven: Yale University Press, repr. Hamden, CT: Archon Books, 1972

Shakespeare, William (1974). "Troilus and Cressida", in *The Riverside Shakespeare*, ed. G. Blakemore Evans. Boston: Houghton Mifflin

Sinclair, Giles (February 1954). "Chaucer—Translated or Obliterated?", *College English*, 15.5: 272–7

Starko, Alane Jordan (1995). *Creativity in the Classroom: Schools of Curious Delight*. New York: Longman

Thompson, Ann (1978). *Shakespeare's Chaucer: A Study in Literary Origins*. New York: Barnes & Noble Books

Trigg, Stephanie (2002). "The New Medievalization of Chaucer", *Studies in the Age of Chaucer*, 24: 347–54

4

"Cross-voiced" Assignments and the Critical "I"

Moira Fitzgibbons

The assignment described in this essay asks students to take on a fictional voice, as well as to critically analyse literary, scholarly, and student texts. Drawing from my experiences with the project, I contend that: 1) encouraging students to write imaginatively *as* a Chaucerian character can help them develop a more sophisticated sense of the stratagems, risks, and evasions operating within any given speaker's "I"; 2) innovative assignments with a creative component are also beneficial because they often motivate students to work more rigorously with literary texts and scholarly sources; and 3) papers with a creative dimension readily lend themselves to equitable grading on the part of English professors, as long as we make our standards explicit to students and to ourselves.

Originally designed for a course I taught in the spring of 2003 on the works of Geoffrey Chaucer and Christine de Pizan, the "cross-voiced" assignment in its first incarnation asked students to take on the voice of one of Chaucer's speakers in order to revise the ideas of one of de Pizan's, or vice versa. I revised the project in the fall of 2003 for a course dealing exclusively with Chaucer: in this version, all the "cross-voicing" happened between Chaucerian characters or narrators. The two courses varied in place, size, and composition. The first was a twenty-student class at Western Washington University, including two literature MA students and eighteen undergraduate English majors. After moving to a new position at Marist College in New York, I then used the assignment within a Chaucer course involving just six undergraduates, half of whom were English majors.

I used the same basic structure for the project in both cases. While the brief (250-word) passage written in the fictional speaker's voice constituted the heart of the assignment, the project contained many components: prewriting, including a preliminary e-mail exchange with fellow students; the actual cross-voiced passage itself, accompanied by a longer analysis of decisions made within the passage; an in-class presentation; and a take-home exam in which students revised their passages in light of one of their classmates' projects.

Before elaborating on the goals and results of the project, a word on terminology seems appropriate: why refer to the assignment as "cross-voiced"? To take the second part of the term first, the idea of "voice" reflects my sense of the complex interplay between oral and textual modes of communication in Chaucer (and to a lesser, but still significant, extent in de Pizan). As H. Marshall Leicester has argued, *The Canterbury Tales* is "written to be read, but read *as if* it were spoken" (Leicester 1980: 221; see also Zieman's [1997] nuanced discussion of "voys" within the *Tales*). I think my use of "voice" was also influenced by a desire to alert students to the Bakhtinian "polyphony" (1981) operating within these works—the way in which a text like *The Knight's Tale* expresses not just one character's views, but also invokes other literary genres, cultural traditions, and rhetorical forms. Moreover, I designed the assignment hoping that the resulting papers would encompass a wide variety of fictional, scholarly, and student voices.

I liked the "cross" part of the phrase for its kinetic sound—it conveyed the sense of back-and-forth movement between writers and texts that I wanted to highlight. We understand de Pizan differently having read *The Man of Law's Tale*, we understand *The Legend of Good Women* differently having read *The Book of the City of Ladies*, we understand Ovid differently based on his quotation by both writers, and so on. In addition, it's perhaps not inappropriate that "cross-voiced" ends up sounding so much like "cross-dressed". In the first course, there was no way that students could complete the assignment without working closely with the ideas of a writer of a different gender than their own. While this was not the case in the Chaucer-only course, many students still took on the guise of the opposite sex. Perhaps even more important was the fact that students would adopt other roles by writing and analysing the passage—those of a medieval writer, of a scholar in his or her own right, and of an educator sharing insights with the class as a whole. As detailed below, I think these forms of impersonation are central to enriching students' understanding of the personal realm.

Taking literature personally

An overarching goal in many of my courses is to encourage students to try on a new kind of "I"—one generated by dialogue, research, and debate, as well as by personal emotion and creativity. Many college students, even upper-level English majors, come to the classroom with the idea that "I" has no place in written academic analysis. A teacher at some stage of their education presumably told them this rule, and (even more significant) they never forgot it. Why does this rhetorical rule loom so large in their minds? I suspect that many traditional-age students retain this idea because it affirms an adolescent sense of the "inner" self as an authentic, pure place in contrast to the false identities imposed by the outside world, academia included.

This strikes me as an idea worth debunking. I don't want to colonise my students' emotions and experiences, but I do want them to develop a more sophisticated understanding of the self's relationship to society, and to question how, in the words of Mariolina Salvatori, "American culture contains 'the personal,' 'the self,' and 'individual identity,' only to make each untouchable and to place it safely beyond the reach of critical analysis" (Salvatori 1997: 581). Examining this process seems particularly crucial given that many of our students get their information from sources of questionable veracity. Unattributed reports, solipsistic blogs, putative experts: given that these voices in our culture are probably here to stay, I think it is more urgent than ever that we remind our students (not to mention ourselves) of the pressing need to examine carefully a speaker or writer's self-presentation.

At the most fundamental level, asking students to scrutinise a speaker's "I" is just another way to posit the question of how people use language, and how language uses people. In particular, the assignment highlights the importance of two processes central to speaking and writing: *dialogue* and *impersonation*. How is a speaker's "I" dependent upon, and organised around, the real or imaginary presence of a "you"? And where is the dividing line between a person's own ideas and the roles allotted to him or her within society at large? Teaching a critical theory course is one way to get students to consider these questions: another way is to have them impersonate and engage in dialogue with others' voices within their own writing. From the perspective of composition studies, George Otte has argued for the benefits of inviting students to take part in these forms of serious play:

> The point of in-voicing other voices is not to make for risk-free, semi-engaged games of pretend; on the contrary, it's to make apparent the risks of a practice we all consciously enact, speaking the already spoken whether by teachers or TV lawyers, evangelists or advertisements, parents or talk show celebrities. Whatever is said is not just mostly borrowed, but borrowed on interest. (Otte 1995: 154)

By alerting students to strategic "borrowings" at work in the statements of fictional characters, academic writers and themselves, I hope to encourage them to question the anti-intellectualism and relativism that often seems pervasive in contemporary culture: for example, "I just think this is right because it's how I feel." Even as I respect students' emotions and opinions, I think it is entirely appropriate to urge them to consider how their feelings intersect with larger cultural questions and exchanges.

These considerations are especially apt within a Chaucer class. Indeed, it would seem absurd to read *The Canterbury Tales* and *The Legend of Good Women* without considering how the narrators and speakers within these works emerge via dialogue with literary traditions, philosophical texts, other characters, and so on. Language as role-play also seems essential to Chaucer's works, especially (though by no means exclusively) the *Tales*. As Leicester has written, "The tales . . . concentrate not on the way pre-existing people create language, but on the way language creates people. They detail how what someone says 'impersonates' him or her, that is, turns the speaker into a person" (Leicester 1980: 217). Instead of considering how the Miller's profession or appearance influence the story he tells, we should draw from the tale itself our sense of who the Miller might be. The same is true for de Pizan, who manifests her own fascination with impersonation; within *The Book of Fortune's Transformation*, for example, her female narrator is granted a strong male body so that she might steer her own "ship" of life.

Students in the Chaucer and de Pizan course were eager to analyse such moments. For its part, the cross-voiced assignment provided participants in both courses with ample opportunities to explore medieval writers' self-transformations. It is impossible for me to evaluate whether or not the project led students to interrogate their own ontological status; the assignment didn't ask them to directly reflect on it, and it didn't come up on course evaluations. I can, however, assert that on the whole students in both courses proved skilful at exploring the different versions of "I" employed by Chaucer (and in the first course, de Pizan).

The cross-voiced passage written by Maureen Mullen, a student in the Chaucer and de Pizan course, worked on this issue in particularly intriguing ways.[1] Mullen envisioned Reason, Rectitude, and Justice encountering the Wife of Bath at the beginning of *The Book of the City of Ladies*, instead of de Pizan's narrator. In Mullen's view, Chaucer would depict the Wife as unwilling to take part in the whole enterprise, acquiescing only to the ladies' recommendation that she refer to herself as "I, Alisoun" (drawing from de Pizan's use of "I, Christine" in *The Book of the*

City of Ladies and other works). The Wife proceeds to use this appellation *ad nauseam* as she bitterly recounts her imprisonment by the three ladies:

> For days Reason visited me, constantly demanding that I, Alisoun give up one pleasure or another due to my widowhood . . . I, Alisoun could imagine [her] prancing around in my moist footwear while I, Alisoun was ensnared behind bars instructed to pray for the departed souls of my husbands.

In her analysis Mullen explained that her passage reflected her sense that Chaucer would make comic fodder out of the complicated acts of self-naming and witnessing performed by de Pizan in her texts. Mullen's work thus indicated how assertions of selfhood can be resisted or "complexly revoiced" (Crane 2002: 3) by readers and writers in order to suit their own ways of seeing the world.

In the vast majority of papers for both courses, students also succeeded in taking on a scholarly "I" that moved well beyond personal intuition in its arguments. In hopes of facilitating this, I photocopied the cross-voiced passages produced by each participant and redistributed them as a booklet so that students could accurately cite them in their take-home final at the end of the term. Even this amateur form of "publication" seemed to encourage students to take their peers' and their own ideas more seriously, and to explore the permeability of different textual voices. This latter practice especially came to the fore in the take-home final of Carrie Goodfellow, a student in the Chaucer and de Pizan course. A classmate had argued that in de Pizan's hands, the Wife of Bath would become a decorous advocate of wifely submission. Responding in her take-home to the student's passage imagining this transformation, Goodfellow asserted that her classmate had distorted de Pizan's ideas:

> [The student] took de Pizan's words on matrimony literally and pre-sented an unfeeling de Pizan who informed us that it was a wife's duty to stand by her husband no matter what he did. In what I felt was a very ingenious move [the student] presented the voice of de Pizan as the Wife of Bath but with an extra twist. Interestingly enough I feel the voice that really comes through in his passage is the mocking voice of Chaucer . . .

The multiple levels of "voicing" get quite elaborate here: according to Goodfellow, the student merged his sensibility with Chaucer's, even as he ostensibly took on de Pizan's mode of writing. The student's resulting revision of the Wife of Bath's "Prologue" reflects not de Pizan's actual concerns, but the way Chaucer might picture de Pizan's revising his own work. Goodfellow's analysis raises fascinating questions: does Chaucer become "ours" when we work with him, or do we become Chaucer's? Equally interesting to me was the fact that the take-home assignment enabled Goodfellow to develop a more confrontational "I" than she had ever used in class discussion: her take-home was a surprise to me, since she had remained silent during the student's presentation.

In fact, I would have to say that within the first course the in-class presentations provided the most disappointing results in my efforts to encourage the students to take on a new "I." Though the cross-voiced passages were quite strong, the question-and-answer period was perfunctory. Perhaps influenced by spring fever or end-of-term exhaustion, most members of the class remained within their roles as students who had fulfilled an assignment and now only wanted to be released from class. Given the chance to redo things, I would probably assign a "designated sceptic" for each presenter—someone required to ask a question at the end of the reading that would indicate how the presenter's ideas might be expanded upon or revised. I have used this technique in other courses involving in-class presentations, and it would seem particularly appropriate to assign students yet another kind of "role" within discussions of this project.

On the other hand, this strategy was not needed in the second course; in this case, the students reacted energetically to one another's passages. The small size of this course may have prevented students from feeling as if they could safely tune out, or perhaps the winter weather proved less of a distraction than the prospect of summer did for the other set of students. In any case, it was particularly gratifying to see students answering one another's questions and responding to one another's work in person. Developing poise is not a skill I necessarily list on my syllabi as a desired outcome for students in my English courses, but perhaps I should: helping students refine their personae as public speakers provides yet another way for them to move beyond solipsism.

Even a troublesome situation within this second course ultimately confirmed for me the benefits of having students share their material with one another in person. One course participant wrote a passage that substituted imitation for impersonation: his revision of *The Knight's Tale* in the voice of the Miller sounded painfully like bad Monty Python. His classmates first responded with silence, then asked a few pointed questions about how the passage might reflect specific parts of Chaucer's actual writing. It was not a particularly comfortable moment, but I think it was a productive one. The student's take-home was a much more fully thought-out piece of writing, suggesting that he had heeded his peers' tacit criticism.

Based on my opposing experiences with these two courses, then, I would continue to advocate the presentation component of the assignment as a *potentially* useful way to help students regard themselves as contributors to an academic community, rather than simply as the reactive half of a one-to-one transaction between professor and student.

Of course, asking students to take on the stance of a scholarly "I" has implications not just for them, but for me as well. As the following two sections should make clear, I think this process requires careful negotiation on my part. I need to maintain a balance between privileging student spontaneity and creativity on the one hand, and providing them with information and guidance on the other. I find this interplay of teaching modes very invigorating, despite (or because of) the fact that it highlights the need to keep my own self-critical "I" in good working order.

The academic imagination

One component of the assignment that makes it somewhat unusual is its combination of critical analysis with "creative" writing. The scare quotes here indicate my sense that there is a strong imaginative component to conventional academic analysis; conversely, writing poetry and fiction necessitates a keen critical acumen. At the same time, I do not think my students are misguided when they perceive a significant difference between writing *about* Chaucer and writing *as* Chaucer. In the section to follow I will argue that asking students to employ the latter mode of writing is greatly beneficial to their execution of the former.

I should state from the outset that I think there are many reasons to privilege creative *writing* projects over those encouraging students to produce their own versions of medieval dress, food, drama, and so on (appealing examples of these kinds of assignments can be found in Curran [1980], Beidler [1996], and the "Feasts and Faires" section of Daniel T. Kline's Chaucer Pedagogy Page on the Web). While I accept Lee Patterson's point that such assignments can usefully "define the cultural space of the class as by rights open to all members" (Patterson 1996: 518), I would not use them as a final project with which to cap my Chaucer course: I think there are many ways to retain a sense of flexibility and accessibility within literature courses while still focusing on reading and writing themselves. For an assignment that invites students to write in the pilgrims' voices (but does not involve engagement with scholarly sources) see Portch (1980). Curran (1980) and Patterson (1996) also offer innovative ways for students to write about/as the pilgrims. See also the "Creative Assignments" section of Kline's Chaucer Pedagogy page. Writing ten years ago in the special *Exemplaria* colloquium on Chaucer pedagogy, Thomas Goodman expressed concern about the way literacy in Middle English seemed to be "slipping away" as a skill gained by undergraduates and emphasised by professors (Goodman 1996: 461). Such developments are especially unfortunate since, as Goodman points out, reading Chaucer can expose students to "the pleasures of new kinds of literacy" (1996: 471).

Goodman's ideas regarding the problems and the opportunities posed by teaching Chaucer strike me as even more pertinent in today's point-and-click culture. To be sure, the Web allows professors and students to mine the riches of such sites as Larry D. Benson's Chaucer website, the *SAC* Online Bibliography, or Daniel T. Kline's Chaucer Pedagogy Page (among many others). At the same time, it also makes available a daunting supply of fool's gold, often offering little to help students recognise distinctions among sources. Given the relatively brief span of time I have with my students, I hesitate to relinquish any opportunity to help them develop the intellectual discipline needed to sort through Middle English verse and Chaucerian rhetoric, to identify and work with scholarly resources beyond those given in a general Google search, and to set forth a cogent argument.

Relatively recent technological change also feeds my interest in assignments that move beyond close reading and literary research, though both skills are called for in the cross-voiced project. As is well known, the Web abounds with resources that are all too amenable to plagiarism. A quick trip to "gchaucer.com," to take just one example, offers for sale dozens of Chaucer-themed essays covering everything from "Religion and Chaucer's Wife of Bath" to "A Theoretical TV Symposium on Women with Barbara Walters" (guest list: Chaucer, Cervantes, and St Augustine, among others). In addition, students need not pay anything to access the comprehensive—if pedestrian—analyses of works like the *Tales* on such sites as "SparkNotes.com." Although devices for detecting Web plagiarism are available, English departments may not have the funds to subscribe to them, and professors may not have the time or desire to police their students' work. Changing the assignments themselves allows us to move beyond a purely defensive response to these challenges.

Moreover, the assignments bring many positive results on their own merits. Generally speaking, the cross-voiced project seemed to generate a kind of productive anxiety in my classes. Students in both courses reported that they found themselves thinking about the assignment while sitting in their other classes. In particular, the same upper-class English majors who could churn out a ten-page analysis with little or no difficulty seemed particularly rattled by the assignment. I think the imaginative dimension of the project heightened the stakes for students, since contemporary culture still tends to associate creative writing with profound emotion and quasi-supernatural inspiration. Rather than explicitly questioning this set of assumptions, I hoped the assignment would do the work for me. To be sure, each student worked with a character or passage that "spoke to" them personally in some way; at the same time, however, they also needed to place their cross-voiced passages in dialogue with a variety of other sources. I hoped their fascination with creative writing would provide fresh stimulus for their work with other kinds of texts.

For the most part, this goal was fulfilled by students' projects. In order to write the cross-voiced passages, many students reexamined citations and allusions within the original literary texts. The student who incurred Carrie Goodfellow's critical ire, for example, framed his passage around the reference to Metellius in the Wife of Bath's "Prologue." Close reading was another key part of the critical portion of the students' papers, and productively informed their decisions within the cross-voiced passage. For Jenne Spano, a student in the second course, working carefully through the Miller's description of Alisoun generated her suggestion that he would transform the Man of Law's Custance into a carnally minded, unreliable woman called Waverly.

Students' conceptualisations of genre also seemed to benefit from the fact that they needed to choose one in order to write their cross-voiced passage. This was especially true for students in the second course. I had been a bit anxious that students in this Chaucer-only class would focus solely on "the personal drama of the pilgrims" (Benson 1986: 148)—that is, that they would become so engrossed with the individual mindsets of the speakers that they would ignore questions of genre, style, and literary precedent crucial to understanding the *Tales*. In the event, however, working just with one author gave students a bit more time and space to consider these issues. A particularly effective treatment of genre was Lauren Ducatelli's paper, which explored how the end of *The Franklin's Tale* might change if it were told by the Miller. Transforming the tale's conclusion into a fabliau, Ducatelli's Miller pictured Dorigen and Aurelius engaging in eager loveplay. Eventually, ill-timed interruptions by both the philosopher and Arveragus cause the scene to devolve into farcical mishaps. Conversely, Kara Shier's passage proposed a variety of strategies that the Knight as a teller might use to clamp down upon the fabliau's subversive possibilities within *The Miller's Tale*. Her Knight transformed John into a self-possessed arbiter of justice, and repositioned Alisoun as a prize to be won in a contest of local carpenters.

These projects also revealed students' openness to scholars' arguments when devising the creative part of their paper. While analysing her passage, Ducatelli described how Thomas J. Farrell's ideas (Farrell 1989) regarding the exposure of private events within fabliaux had led her to believe that the Miller would want to publicly mock Dorigen's and Aurelius's desires, as well as the Franklin's own flawed understanding of nobility. Similarly, Shier wrote that Katherine Zieman's description of the Knight as "obsessed with order" (Zieman 1997: 73) led her to adopt a measured tone and resolve events tidily when she took on the Knight's voice. For students in both courses, their individual investment in the creative dimension of the assignment made them more attentive to critics' ideas than they might otherwise have been. A relativistic attitude toward scholarly arguments (for example, "everyone is entitled to his own opinion") is harder to maintain, I would argue, once a student has committed to shaping a fictional voice in a particular way. Numerous useful strategies for encouraging students to see themselves as *participants* in scholarly discourse can be found in Gaipa (2004).

I did feel, however, that this benefit was a redundant one for the two Master's students in the Chaucer and de Pizan course. In retrospect, I should have asked these students to perform more conventional scholarly analyses. At the postgraduate level, I think most students are sufficiently invested in academic argument that they do not need the extra incentive supplied by papers with a creative component. For these two students—excellent thinkers and writers both—the passage may have served more as a distraction than as an aid to their efforts to develop scholarly voices of their own.

At an undergraduate level, however, the barrier between imaginative and analytic work remains substantial enough that asking students to work in both modes was a good idea. Some adventurous students then began to question other boundaries as well. This was particularly noteworthy in the case of John Elias, a student in the Chaucer and de Pizan course who throughout the semester had contributed to the class by comparing these writers' personae to the alter egos adopted by rap and hip-hop musicians. Performed as a rap, his cross-voiced passage blended verse with a drum track and a sample of fifteenth-century French music that he happened to come across in his collection of LPs (!). In his presentation and in the analytic part of his paper, Elias compared manifestations of misogyny in fourteenth-century poetry with those in twenty-first-century popular music, and considered the connections between hip-hop "sampling" and Chaucer's integration of other poets' work into his texts.

Skilfully assembled and thoughtfully analysed, Elias' passage explored the artistic interplay between medieval and modern forms of creativity, as well as between canonical and popular art (perhaps demonstrated when a colleague in an adjoining classroom demanded volume modulation with a fury that he might not have expressed toward Vivaldi). It also, however, posed some challenges for me as a professor: how exactly should I grade this performance in comparison to the work produced by other students? Undoubtedly, appealing to students' creativity can raise thorny assessment issues, even as it generates exciting work. My experience suggests that careful management of criteria and expectations can do a great deal to allay these problems.

Evaluating challenges

While I hoped the project would strike students as innovative and enjoyable, it also was something that students needed to take seriously: the passage and accompanying analysis were worth thirty per cent of their final grade, and the take-home was worth twenty per cent. The importance of the assignment to students' final grades led me to organise it primarily as an individual effort, rather than as a group project. Although I have had good results asking groups of students in other courses to put on a scene from a medieval drama, "translate" a particular poem into another artistic medium, and so on, I still prefer to evaluate students' most heavily weighted papers on an individual basis. I have never found a way to adequately account for the varying levels of effort that group members bring to a project, or to organise assignments so that students with time-consuming responsibilities outside of class are not placed at a distinct disadvantage. An *exchange* of ideas among students was a key part of the project in both courses, but students did not depend on one another to do one another's research and writing. Several problems that cropped up in both courses with the assignments' required e-mail exchanges—students not responding to each other, or sending one another hastily-conceived ideas—solidified my sense that individual work is the best way to make use of students' time and energy in a final writing project.

With this in mind, I organised both courses' assignments so that students gradually laid the groundwork for their efforts in the last paper. Students in both classes wrote one brief close-reading paper, then a longer essay incorporating literary analysis with a discussion of one scholarly source found by each student. For this latter paper, I distributed a list of databases and bibliographies through which students could locate relevant critical studies. In this way, I prepared them for work with the three scholarly sources that they were required to incorporate into the analytic part of the assignment.

One thing I did not do with either course was ask students earlier in the semester to experiment with fictional literary voices. I might do this differently the next time around: I can envision asking students to produce some informal attempts at speaking as the Knight, Miller, and so on, just to get them acquainted with this mode of writing. Team-teaching the course with a faculty member specialising in Creative Writing would certainly be an intriguing option, but a course with Chaucer as its primary focus strikes me as a difficult one to integrate with a Creative Writing workshop. A guest lecture by a faculty member on crafting and revising a literary voice might be a more viable option.

A mini-workshop on revision might be especially appropriate, given the assignment's emphasis on the accretion and possible alteration of the project over time. I usually require some element of prewriting for all my students' assignments, in order to lessen the possibility of last-minute writing marathons. The unorthodox nature of this assignment made me particularly eager to provide students with a well-structured framework of prewriting efforts and due dates. As mentioned above, some of the e-mail exchanges did prove problematic, perhaps because these components of the assignment were evaluated according to a looser scale (✓+, ✓, or ✓−, corresponding with the grades A, B, or C) and were counted as part of their classwork grade for the course (that is, the mark reflecting student attendance, participation, and in-class writing). Incorporating them into the grade of the cross-voiced passage/analysis itself (again, worth thirty per cent of the overall course grade) and giving them a standard letter grade probably would have given greater weight to these parts of the project.

The problems and possibilities inherent in having students deliver presentations have been mentioned above. I will only add that while they might be unfeasible in some course settings—large lecture courses or on-line classes—professors should remain open to the possibility that such presentations might mitigate the anonymity of these classes. Perhaps the presentations could provide an occasion for members of an on-line course to gather together and work one time in person; perhaps graduate teaching assistants within a lecture course could incorporate presentations into their recitation sessions. Professors wishing to inject a festive element to the end of the semester could forgo grading the presentations, and have students read their work while fortified with food and drink. For my part, I think grading students for their poise and clarity when speaking to other people is a worthwhile enterprise; my specific criteria are outlined below.

A component of the project that I strongly recommend is the take-home exam, the brief (three- or four-page) paper in which students revise their original cross-voiced passage in light of others students' efforts, and explain their changes and choices. Assembling the passages in a photocopied booklet ensured that students would work carefully with one another's ideas: the assignment for the take-home exam required at least two quotations from other students' texts. In both courses the students responded to one another's passages and revised their original ideas with great openness and perspicacity. Several also commented on the parallels between this mode of "revisionist" writing and the echoes, citations, and admonitions present in the tales themselves. The take-homes were fascinating to read: students on opposite sides of a question often engaged with one another's ideas textually, often enriching their own arguments in the process. I think, in general, that this response paper gives students insight not just into medieval literature, but into the importance of give-and-take to scholarly work itself.

The take-homes recall my original goals as a teacher—encouraging students to bring their "I" into a wider dialogue with others, and to consider how one's own position might be affected by the stances of other people. At the end of the day, of course, I needed concrete and fair standards with which to measure how students had achieved these theoretical objectives. Some of these were easy to codify. The presentation needed to provide an energetic reading of the cross-voiced passage, a coherent narrative of how the student's ideas had developed over the course of working on the project, and thoughtful answers to questions posed by me or the class. The handout accompanying the presentation, as well as every component of the project, needed to be lucidly written and meticulously proofread.

My criteria for the critical component of the paper and the take-home required a bit more explanation, so I distributed handouts laying out my criteria. Both required careful quotation of others' ideas (including literary texts, scholarly works, and other students' papers), with careful attention to such matters as the nuances of Middle English words or the meaning of academic jargon. Students were required to append a Works Cited list to their cross-voiced/critical paper citing scholarly sources in MLA format; in addition, I asked them to consider how each source seemed to be positioning itself in relation to larger critical debates within the field. I also told students to move beyond the fictional frame in the critical part of the paper and the take-home; in other words, I wanted them to consider not just the interplay between characters within the literary works themselves, but also the larger context of Chaucer's (and de Pizan's) audience and of contemporary academic discourse. This is a substantial list of goals, but one that can be clearly conveyed to students and to paper-graders outside the course (if blind or double grading is required by an institution), especially if these skills have been emphasised throughout the semester.

While I think I did a good job explaining my standards to both classes through written handouts and oral instructions, some questions did arise concerning the cross-voiced passages—not insurmountable problems, but issues that I would address more explicitly in a future version of the assignment. Two students in the Chaucer and de Pizan course decided to write their passages in Middle English. Though their efforts were ambitious and partially successful, at times the passages lapsed into a muddled mixture of Modern and Middle English. I think this method is better suited to an assignment in which the class as a whole takes Chaucer's Middle English as its primary focus, so that the features of the language can be fully explored (Jost [2000] offers just this sort of assignment). Since my goals lay elsewhere, I asked students in the second course to steer clear of this method. Within the latter course there was a student whose passage raised another problem: he had basically retold the Wife of Bath's "Prologue" without revising the Wife's voice in that of another character. The student explained in our individual meeting before the due date that he wanted to experiment with Chaucer's metrical style—and he had, indeed, produced well-crafted decasyllabic verse. But his final version of the passage did not fully address the complexity of the Wife's ideas or the possible connections between her and another Chaucerian speaker, and he was unhappy with his grade on the paper. In this case, the student and I did not achieve a common understanding of the relationship between form and content in the project.

With these experiences in mind, I think I would clarify in future versions of the assignment that students' cross-voiced passages should demonstrate: 1) awareness of genre; 2) originality (that is, does the passage consider a connection between speakers not explored fully in class?); 3) techniques used by Chaucer to connect or distance himself from the fictional speaker; 4) consideration of medieval historical or cultural issues that might relate to the passage under consideration; 5) rhetorical strategies used by Chaucer to convey particular views of a character or question. All five of these elements would not need to occupy equal time within the cross-voiced passage, but I would require students to manifest at least partial engagement with most of them, and to elucidate their thought process in their critical analyses of the passages. Again, all of these standards could be distributed in written form and maintained within courses where size or institutional requirements mandate multiple graders.

In the future I would also address some of the questions raised by John Elias' rap. While I would still invite students to bring their artistic skills to bear on the assignment, I would make clear that these efforts would count as part of the "originality" dimension of the assignment, and would not themselves replace the need for considerations of genre and so on. Moreover, I would emphasise to students that they were certainly not required to employ these sorts of methods, perhaps by explaining to them the reasons given above for privileging "writerly" kinds of assignments.

This is, no doubt, a lot to do, and it can all be a bit unsettling. "Actually, it's a pretty weird assignment," one Chaucer and de Pizan student blurted out at the end of twenty minutes' intense discussion of his paper-in-progress, revealing the same mixture of anxiety, interest, and good humour shown toward the project by many of his classmates. We laughed; I explained some of my reasons for designing the assignment as I had; he described the pleasures and difficulties he had encountered in his work on it thus far; and off he went.

Partly a standard question-and-answer session and partly a more collaborative dialogue concerning pedagogy itself, the conversation during that office visit represents just one of many unpredictable and stimulating exchanges generated by "cross-voiced" assignments in my Chaucer classes. Managing the resulting amalgam of medieval, scholarly, and undergraduate voices can be challenging for students and professors alike. But grappling with this sort of complexity is worthwhile, I would argue, because it helps us cast a well-trained critical "I" on Chaucer and on other literary and social evocations of personal experience.

Note

1. Students quoted by name have generously given me permission to cite their work. Many thanks to them, and more generally to all the students at Western Washington University and Marist College who took the courses described here.

Works cited

Bakhtin, Mikhail (1981). *The Dialogic Imagination: Four Essays*, ed. Michael Holquist, trans. Caryl Emerson and Michael Holquist. Austin: University of Texas Press

Beidler, Peter (1996). "Teaching Chaucer as Drama: The Garden Scene in 'The Shipman's Tale' ", *Exemplaria* (Teaching Chaucer in the 90s), 8.2: 485–93

Benson, C. David (1986). *Chaucer's Drama of Style: Poetic Variety and Contrast in the "Canterbury Tales"*. Chapel Hill: University of North Carolina Press

Crane, Susan (2002). *The Performance of Self: Ritual, Clothing, and Identity During the Hundred Years War*. Philadelphia: University of Pennsylvania Press

Curran, Terrie (1980). "The Cultural Context", in *Approaches*, ed. Gibaldi. New York: The Modern Language Association of America: pp. 97–104

Farrell, Thomas (1989). "Privacy and the Boundaries of Fabliau in the 'Miller's Tale' ", *English Literary History*, 56.4: 773–95

Gaipa, Mark (2004). "Breaking into the Conversation: How Students Can Acquire Authority for their Writing", *Pedagogy*, 4.3: 419–37

Gallop, Jane, ed. (1995). *Pedagogy: The Question of Impersonation*. Bloomington: Indiana University Press

Gibaldi, Joseph, ed. (1980). *Approaches to Teaching Chaucer's Canterbury Tales*. New York: The Modern Language Association of America

Goodman, Thomas (1996). "On Literacy", *Exemplaria* (Teaching Chaucer in the 90s), 8.2: 459–72

Jost, Jean E. (2000). "Teaching *The Canterbury Tales*: The Process and The Product", *Studies in Medieval and Renaissance Teaching*, 8: 61–9

Kline, Daniel T. (2005.27.12). *The Electronic Canterbury Tales* http://hosting.uaa.alaska.edu/afdtk/ect_main.htm

Leicester, H. Marshall (1980). "The Art of Impersonation: A General Prologue to *The Canterbury Tales*", *Publications of the Modern Language Association of America*, 95: 213–24

Otte, George (1995). "In-voicing: Beyond the Voice Debate", in *Pedagogy*, ed. Gallop. Bloomington: Indiana University Press: pp. 147–54

Patterson, Lee (1996). "The Disenchanted Classroom", *Exemplaria* (Teaching Chaucer in the 90s), 8.2: 513–45

Portch, Stephen R. (1980). "A New Route Down Pilgrims' Way: Teaching Chaucer to Nonmajors", in *Approaches*, ed. Gibaldi. New York: The Modern Language Association of America: pp. 116–20

Salvatori, Mariolina (1997). "Review: The Personal as Recitation", *College Composition and Communication*, 48: 566–83

Zieman, Katherine (1997). "Chaucer's Voys.", *Representations*, 60: 70–91

5
Teaching the Language of Chaucer

Louise Sylvester

When this book was in its earliest planning stages, my co-editor suggested that, since my work has been largely on Middle English lexis, I should contribute a chapter on teaching Chaucer's language. At the time, this seemed a reasonable suggestion; what emerged from my investigation, however, is that Chaucer is rarely approached via the language or in a linguistics context, and that teaching Chaucer's language is generally mentioned only in passing in the descriptions of the most innovative teaching projects that were described in the session at the New Chaucer Society congress and are described in this volume. All this has led me to believe that the idea of teaching the language of Chaucer in British universities in the twenty-first century is one that needs to be problematised rather than described.

Disciplinary and institutional backgrounds

Even before we get to the question of how to devise a course specifically on the language of Chaucer, we need to think about the nature of the degree programme that undergraduate students are likely to be pursuing. As an undergraduate studying English Language and Literature in the 1980s, language study was an essential component of my degree. Some of the language courses on offer were tailor-made for students who were, in essence, taking a degree in English literature; these included, for example, The Language of Shakespeare. Other course options, such as Child Language Acquisition, look like the kind of thing that might now appear on an English Language undergraduate degree course. These language courses bore no overt relationship to the literature curriculum, and sat uneasily in the degree programme as it was then configured; that is, as a chronological route march from Old English to Modernism.

At that time it was not unusual for all language courses to be taught by the medievalists in the department since students studying the elements of Anglo-Saxon needed to become familiar with the concepts of nouns and verbs and the ways that they are conjugated. Basic grammar was taught as part of the medieval literature courses which were usually placed in the first year of the degree. The advantage of this arrangement for the medievalists was that their subject continued to be taught to large numbers of students even when modular degrees and student choices were introduced, since in most places more or less everything taken in the first year was compulsory (as it still is in many institutions). The possible disadvantage was that students were immediately confronted with literature in an incomprehensible language, the teaching of which was unlike that in most other parts of their degree, because it included the need to understand and learn some vocabulary and linguistic structures thoroughly and to undergo the rigours of class tests. Teachers on English language programmes are still struggling with this problem: how to win the hearts and minds of students at the beginning of their degrees, while offering them training which will enable them to do more advanced, and rewarding, linguistic work later on. Discussing the teaching of literacy in Middle English, Thomas A. Goodman (1996) observes that teaching basic skills in any language is not much fun for instructors. Having just spent a semester teaching an introduction to English morpho-syntax I might dispute that, but I guess that such teaching may not be much fun for instructors who are invested in literature rather than in the teaching of language and linguistics.

The issue of teaching the language of Chaucer is, I believe, intimately tied up with the institutional structures in which it takes place. Goodman's (1996) discussion highlights the situation in the United States where many graduate programmes in English and American literature have done away with what were once standard requirements in medieval literature and the history of the English language, and where courses such as Old English regularly fail to make minimum allowable enrolment. On the specific question of Chaucer's language, Goodman comments that while Chaucer is sometimes taught in Middle English, almost everything else in the dialects of this period is taught in translation. Teachers of medieval literature are acutely aware of this question of the difference of Chaucer, both in respect to his language, and the symbolic capital that he has accrued.

In a colloquium entitled "Chaucer and the Future of Language Study," Stephanie Trigg observes that her department, officially called the Department of English Language and Literature, is now known as the

Department of English with Cultural Studies (2002, 349–50). Trigg observes that in the second half of the nineteenth century, when the discipline of English was struggling for acceptance in the university sector, medieval literature gained early admission to the syllabus:

> Middle English both named a language, and implied a pedagogic practice that was subject to the rigors of philology, dialectology, palaeography, codicology, and history . . . Chaucer's texts were included under this rubric, but "Chaucer," on the other hand, also enjoyed membership in a longer literary tradition, and a differently ordered syllabus. The pedagogy associated with this tradition seemed much less secure, in those early days, governed as it was by the disciplines of authorial biography, aesthetic evaluation and personal response. (2002: 348)

Trigg argues that for many Chaucerians it is probably still the case that scholarship on Chaucer's language remains in the background; it is brought into play only if it can be produced as evidence for a disputed point or used as a spring-board for critical insights. Trigg's observations about the changing nature of her university department and, though she does not press the connection, the differing attractions of the various kinds of Chaucer scholarship, are mirrored in my own recent experience of teaching at the University of Manchester in the Department of English and American Studies. The staff included several historical linguists, and courses in the grammar and vocabulary of Old and Middle English as well as that of Early Modern English and Jane Austen's English, were offered alongside their literary counterparts. These courses were open to students in the neighbouring department of Linguistics. During a period of institutional upheaval and change in 2003–2004, the English language group left to join their colleagues in Linguistics, and the Department of English and American Studies ratified its decision to offer a BA in English Literature only. One result of this was that Middle English now signified two entirely different things: a course on the language of the period which was part of the BA in English Language and a course on the literature of the period, taught in the Department of English and American Studies. These two courses now had no pretence at any connection with one another.[1]

The place of language in the teaching of Chaucer

We can identify a number of issues, then: the first is concerned with how we teach Chaucer, including the question of the language variety in which he wrote. The second questions the role of language of literature courses in a climate in which studying literary theory is a concomitant of studying literature, and where the study and teaching of English sees its best justification in alliances with the disciplines of history and, more especially, with cultural theory rather than with the study of English language. The changes in literary studies, and the growth of English language as a separate discipline, means that the idea of a Chaucer course may summon up quite widely varying conceptions of what it should be aiming to do. One can look at a number of Chaucer courses taught at universities both in America and in institutions in countries where English is not the first, or even the second language, for example the Hebrew University in Israel, by following the links from Daniel T. Kline's website "Geoffrey Chaucer: The Electronic Canterbury Tales." Typically, Chaucer's language does not feature on such courses. Sometimes mention is made of the fact that Chaucer's work is written in Middle English. This may include statements such as "You are responsible for acquiring a reasonable familiarity with Chaucer's works in the original Middle English" or a course objective such as "To learn to read and to recite Chaucer's variety of Middle English with reasonable fluency and comprehension." One of the courses I looked at includes translation quizzes and recitation as part of the assessment. There are one or two suggestions in the course outlines that may indicate coded reference to Chaucer's language: part of the assessment for one course was "Participation in 'felt difficulty' exercises via e-mail as assigned" and it seems to me at least possible that the area of potential "felt difficulty" in a Chaucer course is the engagement with the language of the texts. Where Chaucer's language is explicitly included in a syllabus, it is present only as an introductory topic in the first or second week of the course. For instance, one course requires, for Week 1, that students read the Introduction in the Riverside Chaucer, "noting especially the sections on language and versification." The consideration of these topics must be fitted in beside further background material, "Chapter One of the Chaucer Companion—'The social and literary scene in England' ": thus the language section on this course takes up only a small part of the reading for one class. On another course, following an introductory week, the topics assigned for the second class are: " 'Philology': language and manuscripts" before the course gets underway with a list of texts to be read each week. These Chaucer courses, even those which explicitly mention language, do not give any suggestions about how an understanding of Middle English is to be achieved. Presumably, the idea is that resisting the lure of translations and reading plenty of Chaucer's texts will produce at least a reading knowledge of Chaucer's language. Perhaps that is all that is hoped for, particularly at undergraduate level, and especially in the light of the historical and cultural knowledge and modern theoretical perspectives which also clamour for space on the syllabus and which are more likely to feature in the essays that are generally a large part of the assessment.

The teaching of Chaucer at universities in the UK (not represented on Kline's Electronic Canterbury Tales website) has been investigated by Rosalind Field whose report on Chaucer teaching in British universities was based on returns by university lecturers and on web research. Field's report includes some discussion of the teaching of Chaucer's language, and what teachers of Chaucer have to say about this is not very encouraging. Field notes that language awareness is an issue that impinges on the teaching of Chaucer: her informants find "increasing resistance to language" and report that language "can be a difficulty and put students off". Field comments that it may be that "the boundary of language competence is continually shifting forwards" and that students who do not study Chaucer may register problems in the study of Shakespeare and Milton. She notes, however, that "there is clearly an issue here with regard to the time available to familiarize students with Chaucer's language." Field suggests that Old and Middle English teaching used to insist on the importance of translating texts and that the move to at least partial assessment by essay has shifted the emphasis in teaching away from the activity of translation. One result of this change is that students may become reliant on published translations or may simply not understand the texts they are reading. The conclusion of Field's report includes some desiderata. Among these, teachers of Chaucer express a wish for the sharing of ideas on teaching Middle English to students "who are only there for the literature" and one respondent would "appreciate ideas about how to inculcate some minimal knowledge of Middle English"; s/he tries "to infiltrate some of this information into the first week (in a way that seems similar to the American Chaucer courses) and thereafter a language topic briefly into each lecture, e.g. *thou* and *ye* difference." The terms in which this pedagogic decision is enacted are suggestive, indicating that engagement with language on a Chaucer course is likely to be unwelcome and must therefore be clandestine. A similar note is struck in Steven Kruger's essay in this volume when he says that he is not ready to capitulate to an approach to Chaucer that deals in stories and characters acquired through reading the *Canterbury Tales* in translation.

The teaching of Middle English

To discover a little more about how Middle English is taught, we may note that there are plenty of courses on English historical linguistics on offer in British and American universities. Scanning the web for history of the language courses in universities in the UK is not as easy as you might think: in contrast to their American counterparts, British institutions seem to be chary about publishing syllabus details. Most of the courses emphasise external history, although many appear to include some training in linguistics. One course (taught at an American university) starts with phonology, phonemic transcription and semantic shift, before moving into a historical survey that begins with Indo-European languages, moves on to Old English, then Middle English and Early Modern English, ending with Present-day English, English around the world, Regional Variation, Ebonics, American slang and the future of English. This is a fuller course than many, but the historical spread that it aims to cover, and the essentially external approach, is typical. The teaching of the history of the English language in European universities has been investigated via an informal survey of teachers of English historical linguistics at European universities that was published electronically. The survey, conducted by Olga Fischer and Niki Ritt, posed the question "What do you think should a European student of English be taught about the history of the language?" The answers encompassed the following topics: history, methods and tools used in historical linguistics, including historical corpora and the *OED*; language change: what it is and how it can be explained and socio-historical aspects of variation; spelling, orthography, the place of English within the Indo-European family, periods in the evolution of English, medieval and renaissance England, and specific aspects of the (internal) history of English (these to include diachronic phonology, morphology, syntax, word-formation, semantics and lexicon) and synchronic period grammars and texts. As with the Chaucer courses, pressure on the syllabus is evident with regard to historical linguistics, and Fischer and Ritt concede that "hardly any real History of English course will be able to cover more than a fraction of the aspects mentioned given the severe limitations of teaching time Historical Linguistics has to cope with within the normal type of English Studies syllabus." One course taught in a British university, though not one which publishes a list of topics on the Web, emphasises language change and the various approaches which seek to explain it, such as child language acquisition, the structure of linguistic systems, and social and stylistic variation. This combination of theoretically-oriented topics reflects the emphases in many of the history of the English language courses taught in the UK, with teachers seeking to include both a narrative about the changes to the language and its shifting roles, and the details of the structure of the language at different periods. The comments by the authors of the European survey about pressure on the syllabus also hold for British universities, with the result that Middle English takes up only a small part of the history of the language course. In my own university's twelve-week history of the English language course, two weeks are allotted to Middle English: one discussing the impact of the Norman conquest and one dealing with synchronic and diachronic variation in Middle English.

It is difficult, if not impossible, to make any connections between the teaching that is going on in history of the English language courses and the aims of the Chaucer courses outlined above. Teachers of Chaucer voice concerns about their students learning Middle English, both in their course outlines and in their responses to Field's inquiry. They are also exercised about the place of Chaucer in the teaching of medieval literature, questioning the purpose of dedicated Chaucer courses, and wondering whether Chaucer's work should be taught as an introduction to medieval literature and/or alongside other fourteenth-century texts. The particular attractions of Chaucer, and his cultural capital, have recently come under scrutiny. Christopher Cannon's book *The Making of Chaucer's English*, for example, offers a challenge to the traditional view of Chaucerian innovation in respect of the lexicon of English, and his essay on Chaucer's style performs a similar function for that aspect of Chaucer's language use. Wendy Scase, contributing to the colloquium "Chaucer and the Future of Language Study," describes the tradition of regarding Chaucer's English as "modern" while other medieval texts are seen as quite different. Scase notes that this attitude is apparent in publishing policies and pedagogic practices; she points to the decision by the editors of the *Norton Anthology of English Literature* to print all the Old English and Early Middle English texts, and some later Middle English texts that are perceived as particularly difficult, in modern English translations, whereas Chaucer and a few other later Middle English texts are presented in modernised Middle English and flagged as works which even beginners will be able to read. Scase calls for a cultural move that will "return Chaucer to Middle English, Chaucer's language to the larger systems of cultural production, and medievalists' work to the shaping of an English studies for the future" (2002: 333). This call is reflected in Trigg's statement (in the same forum) that as the power of the canon, and therefore of canonical authors, diminishes we will inevitably witness "a process of Chaucer's progressive 'medievalization,' as he recedes further back into a historical era that must seem more and more alien" (2002: 352). These suggestions would seem to support Field's concerns about the boundaries of linguistic competence and the risk that we will discover too late that students cannot understand the texts that they are (supposedly) reading. We may wish, however, to think harder about whether the ability to read Chaucer's texts (and perhaps those of his contemporaries and immediate predecessors) in their original language varieties is enough of a goal for those who wish to interest students in the study of Chaucer's language. Reading competence seems, in this context, to be a somewhat impoverished ideal.

On the relationship between language and literature in Chaucer teaching

On the shelves of libraries and in Chaucer scholarship and criticism, discussions of Chaucer's language are almost entirely separated from literary and historical analyses of Chaucer's work. The collection of Chaucer criticism edited by Corinne Saunders, for example, contains no chapters on Chaucer's language. The critical anthologies that do address the issue of language do so quite briefly; editors generally consider that one chapter is sufficient to address this task.[2] As we have seen, this division is reflected in course structures. At Towson State University, for example, the same professor teaches courses in Chaucer, Old English, Medieval British Literature and History of the English Language (among others). The Chaucer course begins with "Registration & Introduction" followed by a class on "Middle English Pronunciation & *The Mother Tongue*." The classes that follow cover, serially, *The Canterbury Tales* and *Troilus and Criseyde*. The History of the English Language course includes three weeks on Middle English, and the aims of the course are entirely centred on language study; the course consists of "A study of the origins, changes, and reasons for changes in the grammar, sounds, and vocabulary of English from the beginnings of the language to modern times." It should perhaps be added that the final course objective (aims and objectives appear as separate lists) does mention awareness of English as a vehicle for literary expression, past and present. Interestingly, the Old English course at the same institution aims to "introduce the student to the Old English language through the study of Old English grammar and through readings of Old English prose and poetry." The course objectives here, though, are more concerned with the literature than with the language of Old English. For Middle English, the almost complete separation of the study of language and literature, as evidenced in the course outlines available on the Web, is entirely typical. As we have seen, this separation was reified in the case of Chaucer in particular from the beginnings of English as a university subject.

The question of the connection between the teaching of the history of the English language and medieval literature is discussed by Steen Schousboe in an essay on the teaching of historical linguistics at the University of Copenhagen. Schousboe observes that in his department, as in most other European universities, the teaching of historical linguistics was concomitant with courses in which Old and Middle English texts were studied. Until the growth of language study as a separate discipline, this was standard in most British universities too; as mentioned above, it was thought that it was impossible to teach students to read Old and Middle English literature without their having some understanding of the structures of these language varieties, and thus it fell to the scholars of Ælfric, *Beowulf*, Chaucer and Malory, to teach the basic elements of English grammar. This traditional division of responsibility is reflected in the make-up of some English departments today; at the University of Sheffield, for example, the teaching of the literature of the early modern period and after takes place in the department of English literature, while the teachers of Old and Middle English (language and/or literature) belong to the department of language and linguistics. Schousboe suggests that such teaching arrangements are a legacy of nineteenth-century scholarship and he is keen to separate the teaching of historical linguistics and the teaching of medieval texts. Schousboe's objections are based on the workload that learning to read medieval texts imposes on students; he suggests that it takes a long time, over a year in his opinion, for a student to acquire the necessary fluency in Old and Middle English literature so that historical linguistics took up a considerable portion of the syllabus for these subjects. This ensured a longer lifespan for historical linguistics, but did not, ultimately, provide a justification for its continued space on the syllabus. In the University of Copenhagen, both historical linguistics and the reading of texts in Old and Middle English were abandoned as obligatory disciplines in the mid-1970s. Schousboe, writing from the point of view of a historical linguist, suggests that for today's students, the constant use of a dictionary and a grammar to get through a text is an unfamiliar discipline, especially given the changes to the teaching of modern languages that have taken place. He concludes that the heavy reliance on reading "authentic" texts became a millstone round the neck of historical linguistics and that, in his institution at least, "it would be futile to try to revive the teaching of historical linguistics without ridding it of that millstone."

Many of the disciplinary structures, as reflected in the current organisation of English departments in British universities, suggest that there is considerable support for the unyoking of the teaching of the history of the English language from the study of medieval literary texts. Linguists want to develop their own discipline; indeed, many have called for the integration of relatively new subdisciplines of linguistics into the teaching of historical linguistics, suggesting that ideas from cognitive linguistics, for example, could play a productive part in the study and teaching of language change. The suggestions of Schousboe and others signal a move away from the focus on philology and phonology that were characteristic of historical linguistics as it used to be taught in conjunction with medieval literature. Similarly, as we have seen, teachers of Chaucer wish that their students had time to develop their skills in reading Middle English, but most teachers also want to include literary (and non-literary) theory in their courses; they wish to take account of feminist readings of Chaucer, for example, or to apply psychoanalytic or postcolonial theory, which their students might encounter on courses dealing with more recent cultural productions, to the study of Chaucer.

It is certainly not the case, however, that all universities want to align themselves with the disseverance of literature and language. At the University of Sheffield, an option entitled The Language of Power is part of the course offerings in the Department of English Literature, while at my own university there are a number of courses which seek to integrate the study of language and literature. There is a third-year option, for example, entitled Literary Linguistics. It is evident that some scholars believe that the loss of language study from the teaching of Chaucer would involve an impoverishment of understanding. In the preface to *The Language of Chaucer*, David Burnley suggests that the book is addressed "rather to the reader of Chaucer than to the student of language," implying that these are separate communities of scholars and students. He goes on to observe, somewhat wistfully, however, that the book's "ideal audience would be that reader who would seek to make no distinction between the two activities." A connection between knowledge of Chaucer's language and sensitive textual reading is the major theme of Burnley's book; he argues, for example, that the relative ease with which we can read Chaucer may cause us to miss the different meanings and connotations which familiar-seeming words and phrases may have, and to skip over puzzling grammatical constructions. These two dangers may lead us into literary interpretations which are dependent on "that incomplete text which is created by our desire to read faster than unrecognised difficulties will properly permit" (1983: 10). Similarly, he later observes that "although Chaucer's language is, in outline, similar to modern English, it is to be expected that . . . there will be discrepancies which coarsen our appreciation of his meaning" (1983: 39). These remarks may be seen as simply indicating what is at stake in students acquiring an ability to read Chaucer's language. Certainly they underline the need for careful reading of the original language of the texts. Part of Burnley's project is to investigate what he terms the "architecture" of Chaucer's language. This includes understanding both the "connotational" meaning and the cognitive meaning of Chaucer's vocabulary choices: the latter being the sense in context of a word, or its primary sense when out of verbal context; the former, the memories of other senses and other circumstances of the use of a word beyond the usage under investigation (1983: 208). Burnley's proposals may be seen, too, as early statements of the move outlined above that seeks to locate Chaucer's language in its medieval context. This move is paralleled, however, by the desire by teachers of the history of the English language to bring recent linguistic approaches, for example cognitive linguistics, or sociolinguistics, to bear on historical linguistics.

Teaching the language of Chaucer

There is not space in this essay to imagine in detail a course on the language of Chaucer which would answer the desires of literary and linguistic scholars, varied disciplinary and institutional demands, what students think they want, and what different kinds of teachers want for them. Nevertheless, I should like to indicate some approaches that might result in interesting and productive lines of inquiry.

One important suggestion is that integrating more recent approaches to the study of language, such as sociolinguistics, into the discipline of historical linguistics, would enable us to reinstate Chaucer in his linguistic context; that is, he would come into focus as a medieval author writing in the language which he had inherited and making use of the linguistic forms of the social milieux that he inhabited. We need to enact what Scase calls the cultural move; that is, the analysis of Chaucer's linguistic practice (and that of other medieval authors), contextualised within "the linguistic system as a whole, and in the light of what the users and shapers of that system knew about its meanings and its implications as a social practice" (2002: 328). Scase identifies pragmatics, that is the study of the meanings that speakers understand, rather than the semantics of utterances, as a framework for such an analysis. This approach is adumbrated in her consideration of the *Reeve's Tale* in which, she suggests, Chaucer both deploys the varieties and registers of English alongside one another to achieve ironic and humorous effects, and also attributes to certain characters an awareness of the pragmatics of the language, an understanding of, and an attempt to exploit, its social and situational meanings (2002: 332). It would, I think, be all too easy for students to take on the latter part of this suggestion, without gaining any real understanding of what we know about the language of Chaucer's time and place, and of how we arrive at the knowledge that we have. Here, a course on the language of Chaucer might dovetail with some of the expressed aims of a course in historical linguistics. Students could be introduced to the major research tools: the *Middle English Dictionary* (on-line, preferably), the *Oxford English Dictionary*, and the *Linguistic Atlas of Late Medieval English*, for example, as well as machine-readable corpora. Students would gain both an introduction to corpus linguistics, and a sense of the work that has been done to reconstruct Chaucer's linguistic setting.

Scase's work is suggestive about the social context of Chaucer's language. For a deeper understanding of this, students could be introduced to the ideas derived from sociolinguistics that have been mapped on to historical linguistics producing a sociohistorical linguistic approach. As Jeremy Smith suggests, the foundation of such understanding comes from paying attention to the communicative functions fulfilled by English in the Middle English period (see Smith 1996; 2002; Horobin & Smith 2002; Smith forthcoming).[3] It is only by considering the shift in the range of the functions of the vernacular which took place during the Middle Ages that we can analyse language attitudes to English during the time that Chaucer was writing. Students can be introduced to the beginnings of standardisation and encouraged to think about the ways that standardisation produces understanding of what constituted prestige forms together with shifting attitudes to nonstandard forms. They may then begin to think about the rise of accent as a social symbol.

Smith suggests that we must generate an understanding in students that they need both an awareness of the linguistic resources available to authors in terms of lexis, grammar, and sound- and writing-systems and also a sense of how these levels of language were harnessed within the stylistic and sociolinguistic traditions current at the time. Equally, they need to examine how Chaucer, as an individual author, engaged with these materials (2002: 335). Smith is thus indicating a further framework, one rooted in stylistics, following a model which is suggested in Burnley's work. A course taking this approach to Chaucer's language would introduce students to some of the basic concepts in stylistics: textual cohesion, achieved through the use of pronouns and the definite article, conjunctions, ellipsis and lexical choices; modality; shifts in speech reporting between direct and indirect speech, for example, and showing how Chaucer's use of these stylistic possibilities differs from that of his contemporaries, and from writers working in later periods. Another area of interest that is linked to both sociolinguistic and stylistic approaches is that of register and propriety. Considering Chaucer's awareness of these would encourage students to think about Chaucer's vocabulary, its origins and use by Chaucer and the usages of his immediate predecessors as well as those who came after him. Linguistic ornamentation would be one focus here, complemented by the study of comments on Chaucer's use of it that are found in the work of later writers such as Dunbar (see Smith 2002: 336). Another avenue which could be explored is Chaucer's representation of the different modes demanded by the various genres he employs. Both areas of exploration would offer students a sense of what we mean by style: the particular thumbprint of an author that means that we recognise his or her writing whenever we come across it, and, at the same time, the idea of style contained in our definitions of register: what, for example, does Chaucer wish to evoke when he speaks of "stile" or of "heigh stile." All these ideas would, I think, prove interesting to students and could be taught either as a prerequisite to a more conventional Chaucer course; as a follow-up to such a course; or, alongside other approaches, taking those parts of the linguistics programme which seem most appropriate to the discussion of individual texts. It seems clear that the time has come to reimagine the relationship between language and literature in our approach to teaching Chaucer.

Notes

1. This solution did not please everybody, however: one professor, who works across the language/literature boundary, left the university because of a wish to continue to work on language while retaining the link with literature.
2. See, for example, Donka Minkova's chapter in Steve Ellis's Oxford guide to Chaucer which takes up twenty-seven pages of a 644-page volume, and Chapter 2 of Margaret Hallissy's Chaucer companion which runs from p. 9 to p. 14 of a 318–page book. The latest edition of the *Cambridge Companion to Chaucer* edited by Piero Boitani and Jill Mann has one chapter which addresses linguistic issues, Christopher Cannon's "Chaucer's Style."
3. I am grateful to Professor Smith for letting me have a copy of his chapter "From Middle to Early Modern English" ahead of publication.

94   *Teaching Chaucer*

Works cited

Besserman, Lawrence (2005.27.12). *Chaucer: The Canterbury Tales*
   http://micro5.mscc.huji.ac.il/~english/44970Syllabus.pdf
Boitani, Piero & Jill Mann, ed. (2003). *The Cambridge Companion to Chaucer*, 2nd
   edn, Cambridge: Cambridge University Press
Burnley, David (1983). *A Guide to Chaucer's Language*. Basingstoke: Macmillan—
   now Palgrave Macmillan
Cannon, Christopher (1998). *The Making of Chaucer's English: A Study of Words*.
   Cambridge: Cambridge University Press
———. (2003). "Chaucer's Style", in *Cambridge Companion to Chaucer*, ed. Boitani &
   Mann: pp. 233–50
Duncan, Edwin (2005.27.12). *History of the English Language*
   http://www.towson.edu/%7Educan/helinfo.html
———. (2006.15.1). *Chaucer* http://www.towson.edu/~duncan/chauhom3.html
———. (2006.15.1). *Old English*
   http://www.towson.edu/~duncan/475home.html
Ellis, Steve, ed. (2005). *Chaucer*. Oxford: Oxford University Press
Field, Rosalind (2005). *Chaucer Teaching in UK Universities*
   Retrieved on 2005.27.12 from:
   http://www.oup.com/uk/booksites/content/0199259127/resources/
   ukuniversities.pdf
Fischer, Olga & Niki Ritt (2005.27.12). *A Core Curriculum for Teaching English
   Historical Linguistics at European Universities*
   http://www.univie.ac.at/Anglistik/hoe/cc.htm
Goodman, Thomas (1996). "On Literacy", *Exemplaria* (Teaching Chaucer
   in the 90s):
   http://web.english.ufl.edu/exemplaria/sympo.html#goodman
Hallissy, Margaret (1995). *A Companion to Chaucer's Canterbury Tales*. Westport,
   CT and London: Greenwood Press
Historical Linguistics, Linguistics Tripos: Paper 7 and Preliminary Paper 7, MML
   Part 2: Paper Li7
   http://www.mml.cam.ac.uk/ling/courses/ugrad/p_7.html
Horobin, Simon & Jeremy Smith (2002). *An Introduction to Middle English*.
   Edinburgh: Edinburgh University Press
Kline, Daniel T. (2005.27.12). *The Electronic Canterbury Tales*
   http://hosting.uaa.alaska.edu/afdtk/ect_main.htm
Minkova, Donka (2005). "Chaucer's Language: Pronunciation, Morphology,
   Metre", in *Chaucer*, ed. Ellis: pp. 130–57
Morris, Tim (2005.27.12). *History and Development of the English Language*
   http://www.uta.edu/english/tim/courses/4301f98/
Saunders, Corinne, ed. (2001). *Chaucer*. Oxford: Blackwell
Scase, Wendy (2002). "Tolkien, Philology, and The Reeve's Tale: Towards the
   Cultural Move in Middle English Studies", *Studies in the Age of Chaucer*, 24:
   325–34
Schousboe, Steen (2005.27.12). *Teaching Historical Linguistics*
   http://www.univie.ac.at/Anglistik/hoe/pschousboe.htm
Smith, Jeremy (1996). *An Historical Study of English: Function, Form and Change*.
   London: Routledge

———. (2002). "Chaucer and the Invention of English", *Studies in the Age of Chaucer*, 24: 335–46

———. (forthcoming). "From Middle to Early Modern English"

Szarmach, Paul E. (2005.27.12). *Chaucer*
http://www.wmich.edu/medieval/academic/courses/eng555/syllabus.html

Trigg, Stephanie (2002). "The New Medievalization of Chaucer", *Studies in the Age of Chaucer*, 24: 347–54

6
Teaching the Language of Chaucer Manuscripts

Simon Horobin

In this chapter I describe the ways in which I introduce students to the study of the language of Chaucer manuscripts. This subject forms part of an optional course dealing with medieval literature that is offered to students in the third or fourth year of an MA (Hons) degree, specialising in either English Language or English Literature. This course is taken by an average of thirty students each year, all of whom have had some prior encounter with Chaucer and study of his language, although some are interested in Chaucer more as a literary writer while others have an ongoing linguistic interest. Because of the different interests of the student audience my focus is on the literary implications of the linguistic features I discuss, although some of the more specialised issues concerning the London dialect are dealt with in greater detail as part of a course on the History of the English Language offered to approximately thirty fourth-year students studying English Language at Honours level.

The Scottish MA is a four-year Honours degree in which students take a combination of three subjects in their first two years, proceeding to Honours at the end of their second year. In their third and fourth years students pursue either a single or joint honours programme, taking a total of eight courses.

One of the principal reasons for encouraging students to engage with the primary linguistic data supplied by manuscripts of Chaucer's works, rather than rely exclusively on edited texts, is to introduce them to the concept of variation. Linguistic variation is central to an understanding of Chaucer's language and it is therefore important that students are aware of this concept from an early stage in their studies (Burnley 1983). To make students aware of the significance of variation for an understanding of Chaucer's language, I present them with examples of words with variant spellings and ask them to examine their distribution across the *Canterbury Tales* and try to account for their use. This exercise is carried out in the School of English and Scottish Literature's computer laboratory which has access to relevant databases and to software which allows texts to be interrogated in a variety of different ways. Students are divided into pairs and encouraged to work together, sharing their different experience and expertise with information technology and with Chaucer's language. The exercise takes place during a one-hour seminar in which I am present to facilitate and to advise students on their individual projects, although the main focus of the session is on students' hands-on encounter with the primary data. Students are permitted to ask questions of a specific or technical nature, but are expected to tackle the tasks without my intervention. I use this methodology as this material is especially well suited to allowing students to engage with large amounts of data and to interact with each other so as to enable peer learning, important advantages of using ICT (Laurillard 2002). For instance one such exercise includes an examination of the distribution of two variant spellings of the word "hand": *honde* and *hande*. Students are then expected to choose from a variety of databases and electronic corpora the best resource for tackling this problem. In carrying out this exercise they have access to the following databases: *The Glossarial DataBase of Middle English*, which provides complete lists of occurrences of individual words in Chaucer's *Canterbury Tales*, electronic texts of Chaucer's works, available as part of various electronic text collections, the *Middle English Dictionary*, available as part of the Middle English Compendium. Having used these resources to analyse the frequency and distribution of these forms, the students are then expected to suggest reasons for the use of the choice of one variant over another. In a similar task students are asked to investigate variant spellings of words such as *merry, busy, church, hill*, which all had the same vowel sound in Old English. The East Midlands dialect of ME, which included that of London, pronounced this group of words with [ɪ, iː] and spelled them with an <i> or a <y>. In the West Midlands these words were spelled with a <u>, while in the South-East and East Anglia they were spelled with an <e>. As a result of immigration into the capital from these various areas, all three pronunciations and spellings were available in the London dialect and Chaucer used all three. By analysing the distribution of these different spellings across Chaucer's works students discover how he manipulated these variant forms for the purposes of rhyme. These exercises are intended to demonstrate to students how Chaucer could draw on different pronunciations of certain words and how this variation was of considerable benefit to him when selecting rhyme words.

The reason for structuring the course in this way is to encourage students to attempt to account for Chaucer's use of variation for themselves, rather than simply presenting them with a series of examples complete with explanations. Students respond effectively and enthusiastically to such an approach and find that they learn much more from a problem-solving approach rather than from a more traditional lecture format in which they are simply presented with explanations for these phenomena. Following the lab session students present their findings as reports to the entire class of approximately thirty students. Each pair of students is allotted a ten minute slot in which they present their findings and summarise their conclusions. Following this there is a time of questions in which the audience, made up of myself and the other students on the course, ask questions and engage in a more general discussion. This is an important part of the process, as I feel strongly that ICT should not be used as a replacement for teacher–student interaction, but rather to complement and facilitate it (Ramsden 2003). I find that this teaching format, in which students become researchers, interrogating primary data and then reporting their findings to their peers, works particularly well for those students who are studying linguistics courses. These students are often familiar with the procedures involved in carrying out fieldwork, in which informants are selected and interviewed to produce the raw data which is then analysed. While modern linguists interview living informants, the informants that are interrogated by my students are historical texts. This is a helpful analogy as it stimulates them to question the status of their informants and their reliability as evidence of language use.

This leads me to the second major reason why I think it is important to introduce students to the study of Chaucerian manuscripts: the question of evidence. In the exercises described above students rely exclusively on edited texts, such as the *Riverside Chaucer*, without considering what primary evidence lies behind these texts, and their status as witnesses to Chaucer's language. The next stage in this exercise is to confront students with the primary data presented by Chaucer manuscripts, to make them aware of the differences between a fifteenth-century manuscript and a modern printed edition. The earliest and most accurate manuscripts of Chaucer's works are the Hengwrt and Ellesmere manuscripts. It is significant that neither of these manuscripts was produced during Chaucer's lifetime, so that their status as evidence for Chaucer's own language is problematic. It is generally accepted by scholars that the Hengwrt manuscript (Aberystwyth, National Library of Wales MS Peniarth 392D) represents the scribe's first attempt to compile a complete copy of the *Canterbury Tales*. However, most editions of the poem are based upon the slightly later Ellesmere manuscript (San Marino, Henry E. Huntington Library MS EL 26.C.9). This is significant as the text of the Ellesmere manuscript appears to have been edited, so as to reduce or eliminate much of the linguistic variation that we have seen was part of Chaucer's dialect. One of the driving principles behind the production of the Ellesmere manuscript was regularity, so that many of the gaps, inconsistencies and irregularities of the text and arrangement of the Hengwrt manuscript have been carefully ironed out in Ellesmere. This desire for regularity and consistency was also applied to details of spelling, so that the language of Ellesmere is more consistent than that of Hengwrt. A good way of demonstrating this to students, and getting them to identify for themselves the kinds of changes implemented by the Ellesmere editors, is to present them with parallel sections from the two manuscripts. Transcriptions of both manuscripts are now readily available, both in printed and electronic form. The printed facsimile of the Hengwrt manuscript contains a complete transcription of the manuscript, accompanied by a listing of all the variants found in Ellesmere (Ruggiers 1979). More useful for this kind of exercise is the electronic facsimile of Hengwrt which contains complete transcriptions of both manuscripts, with all variants highlighted in red.

In my own teaching I use the electronic facsimile of Hengwrt and present students with extracts from both manuscripts taken from this publication. Working in pairs they are then asked to carry out a detailed comparison of a single passage from both Hengwrt and Ellesmere and to suggest explanations for the differences between them. Each pair of students is given a worksheet that poses a series of questions concerning the texts that they are comparing. The worksheets are handed out in the class and the students then spend the remainder of the time working together on their particular assignment. As an example of the kinds of questions that accompany their comparison of these two manuscripts, and as indication of the kinds of issues that can fruitfully be pursued, here are some sample questions that I use in this format:

Sample questions

Below are extracts from two of the earliest and most important manuscripts of the *Canterbury Tales*.

1. Compare the language of the two extracts and identify any differences in spelling, pronunciation and morphology.
2. Why do you think there are such differences between these two extracts and what do they tell us about Chaucer's language?

3. These two manuscripts were written by the same scribe. What does that suggest about the nature of linguistic variation in Middle English?
4. Compare these two extracts with the equivalent passage in the *Riverside Chaucer*. What changes have been introduced by the editor? Why do you think these changes have been made?

Giving students access to primary data in this way forces them to look beyond the edited texts with which they are familiar and to see what raw manuscript data actually looks like. This exercise also makes them confront the question of the reliability of their informants, especially the edited texts upon which the majority of their study of Chaucer will be based. As well as questioning the reliability of modern edited texts, students are also expected to question the status of manuscripts as informants, comparing them with the informants used in modern linguistic surveys. To do this they are expected to consider the differences between the two processes, and to think about the kinds of background information that is lacking when we analyse a manuscript, compared to that which is known of a modern informant.

Having carried out a comparative exercise of this kind, students are then presented with the same portion of text as it appears in a modern edition of the poem, so that they can see the kinds of changes that are commonly made by editors of Chaucer's works. In this exercise students are presented with extracts from different editions, to help them identify different editorial approaches in the selection of specific readings and treatment of texts. Working in the same pairs, students are then asked to identify the kinds of changes introduced by editors, including features such as modernisation of spelling, word division, punctuation, capitalisation and the removal of variation. Once they have completed these tasks the students are expected to summarise their findings for the rest of the class in a series of short presentations. Following these presentations I then lead a discussion in which we attempt to summarise the various findings in order to construct an overview of how manuscripts differ from each other and the kinds of changes introduced by editors. As the pairs of students have compared their sections of the texts with different editions, this also enables a discussion of different editorial theories and methodologies, and how these affect the presentation of Chaucer's language and their status as linguistic informants.

So far we have focused entirely on two manuscripts of Chaucer, to the exclusion of a large number of surviving copies of his works. When using this material with students taking the History of English course I also show them other manuscripts to introduce the concept of Middle

English dialect variation. The widespread nature of Chaucer's popularity during the fifteenth century means that there are numerous surviving manuscripts of his works copied in a range of different dialects, providing a valuable resource for the study of Middle English dialect variation. There are, for example, over fifty surviving complete manuscripts of the *Canterbury Tales*, copied in dialects encompassing the following regions: London, East Anglia, Kent, the West Midlands and the North. By comparing the language of manuscripts copied in these different dialects students can gain insights into the kinds of changes made by scribes when adapting Chaucer's language for a provincial readership. Once again, I find that the best way of introducing students to the study of dialect variation is by presenting them with parallel texts of a section of the *Canterbury Tales* and encouraging them to identify differences between them. Resources are available to enable this kind of activity, both in printed and electronic formats. The parallel-text transcriptions produced by the Chaucer Society (Furnivall 1868–84) in the nineteenth century are a reasonable starting point, but they are not always accurate and have now been superseded by the CD-ROM editions produced by The *Canterbury Tales* Project. These CD-ROM editions provide transcriptions and digital images of all surviving manuscript and pre-1500 printed witnesses for various parts of the *Canterbury Tales*, enabling quick and easy comparison across the different manuscript versions. To date the Project has published editions of the Wife of Bath's "Prologue", *General Prologue* and the *Miller's Tale*, and further releases are planned for the future (Robinson 1996; Solopova 2000; Robinson 2004). Presenting students with a sample tranche of text in several different manuscript witnesses, enables them to observe for themselves the kinds of differences that distinguish Middle English dialects.

As with the previous exercises, students are grouped in pairs and are encouraged to identify differences between the Hengwrt and Ellesmere manuscripts and another manuscript copied in a different dialect. They are expected to observe such differences and classify them according to the different levels of language: spelling (and pronunciation), lexis and grammar. Spelling changes are by the far most common and easy to identify, though I also try to get students thinking about whether such differences would have affected the way a text was pronounced. This is an important issue and a good way to introduce students to the difficulties in reconstructing how Middle English, and Chaucer's poetry, were pronounced.

As well as identifying differences in spelling and their significance for pronunciation, I also ask students to look for grammatical changes across the manuscript tradition. One interesting grammatical feature to consider is the treatment of adjectival inflexion by Chaucer's scribes. To do this, students use the Wife of Bath's "Prologue" on CD-ROM, employing its collation facility to see how later scribes treat weak and strong adjectives in Chaucer's text. This CD-ROM presents a complete list of variant forms for each individual reading, so that students may calculate the number of scribes who preserve a weak adjective and the number that do not. The students are then expected to use the manuscript descriptions to determine the dates of these manuscripts and to use these to produce a chart showing the process by which this feature of adjectival inflexion was lost. By examining the treatment of this important feature of Chaucer's grammar by later scribes, students gain first-hand insights into the processes of linguistic change, as well as into the understanding and appreciation of Chaucer's metre throughout the fifteenth century.

Changes at the level of lexis are less common in Chaucer manuscripts, presumably because scribes were constrained by the metre and by Chaucer's increasingly authoritative status. However examples of scribes replacing Chaucer's words with others can be found and I also find that it is interesting to encourage students to speculate about the possible reasons behind such changes. To do this I give the students a list of words found in the Wife of Bath's "Prologue" and ask them to use the collation facility on the CD-ROM to identify scribal alternatives, and to suggest explanations for these scribal replacements, taking into account factors such as distinctions in register, style, connotation and etymology. To take full account of these factors students are expected to consult the *Middle English Dictionary*, to consult its definitions, sample citations and etymology, and to search for these words across a range of other Middle English texts, including Chaucer's other works. This enables them to derive a much fuller appreciation of a particular word's status in ME and the likely reasons for its rejection by a particular scribe.[1]

As well as their usefulness as a way of introducing students to ME dialectology, Chaucer manuscripts also contain important evidence concerning the transmission of Chaucer's language. While many scribes replaced aspects of Chaucer's language with their own preferred forms, there is also considerable evidence that scribes were constrained to retain features of Chaucer's language which were felt to be authentically Chaucerian (Horobin 2003). This is particularly apparent when we turn to the end of the fifteenth century, when the process of linguistic change had begun to make Chaucer's language appear outdated and old-fashioned. But rather than simply update Chaucer's language by replacing its archaic forms with more modern ones, scribes frequently retained the archaic forms. So when comparing the language of copies of Chaucer's manuscripts, I also ask students to pay attention to details which do not change and to think about why such there should be such stability. As well as relating to Chaucer's status as an author, the tendency for greater uniformity in the language of these manuscripts is also related to the wider issue concerning linguistic standardisation, a process which has its beginnings in the fifteenth century, and so also provides a way of demonstrating this process in action.

So, by studying the language of Chaucer manuscripts, students become aware of a range of issues concerning Middle English and Chaucer's language which have a relevance for their understanding of Chaucer's works and their subsequent transmission and reception. The resources are now available to enable teachers to encourage students to go beyond the artificial, modernised text of a modern edition and to confront the variety and inconsistency that is found in genuine Middle English texts, and that provided the raw materials for Chaucer's verse. By drawing on these resources and exposing students to genuine Middle English, as opposed to an edited version, they gain important insights into the variation found within Middle English and the reasons behind the choice between variant forms. This is also a useful way of encouraging students not to rely uncritically on modern editions of medieval texts and provoking them to consider the ways in which editors impose regularity and consistency on Middle English texts, and the effect this can have on our reading and interpretation.

Note

1. One way of approaching the treatment of dialect words by Chaucer's scribes that I find particularly fruitful is to look at the representation of the Northern dialect of the two Cambridge students in the *Reeve's Tale*, and how this is transmitted across the manuscript tradition (Horobin 2001). The treatment of the vocabulary in the *Reeve's Tale* is not limited to the replacement of Northernisms by Southern equivalents. Some scribes, clearly appreciating Chaucer's attempt to convey Northern dialect, actually increased the portrayal by adding to the Northern vocabulary.

Works cited

Benson, Larry D. *Glossarial DataBase of Middle English*
   www.hti.umich.edu/g/gloss/
   ———. ed. (1988). *The Riverside Chaucer*. Oxford: Oxford University Press

Burnley, J. D. (1982). "Inflexion in Chaucer's Adjectives", *Neuphilologische Mitteilungen*, 83: 169–77

———. (1983). *A Guide to Chaucer's Language*. Basingstoke: Macmillan—now Palgrave Macmillan

Furnivall, F. J., ed. (1868–84). *The Six-Text Edition of Chaucer's Canterbury Tales*, Chaucer Society, 1st series. London: Trübner

Horobin, Simon (2001). "JRR Tolkien as a Philologist: A Reconsideration of the Northernisms in Chaucer's *Reeve's Tale*", *English Studies*, 82: 97–105

———. (2003). *The Language of the Chaucer Tradition*. Cambridge: D. S. Brewer

Laurillard, Diana (2002). *Rethinking University Teaching and Learning: A Conversational Framework for the Effective Use of Learning Technologies*. London: RoutledgeFalmer

Middle English Dictionary (1952–2001). Ann Arbor: University of Michigan Press

Oxford English Dictionary (1989) 2nd edn. Oxford: Oxford University Press

Ramsden, Paul (2003). *Learning to Teach in Higher Education*. London and New York: Routledge

Robinson, Peter, ed. (1996). *The Wife of Bath's* Prologue on CD-ROM. Cambridge: Cambridge University Press

———. (2004). *The Miller's Tale* on CD-ROM. Leicester: Scholarly Digital Editions

Ruggiers, Paul G., ed. (1979). *A Facsimile and Transcription of the Hengwrt Manuscript, with Variants from the Ellesmere Manuscript*. Oklahoma: Pilgrim Books

Samuels, M. L. (1972). *Linguistic Evolution with Special Reference to English*. Cambridge: Cambridge University Press

Solopova, Elizabeth, ed. (2000). *The General Prologue on CD-ROM*. Cambridge: Cambridge University Press

Stubbs, Estelle, ed. (2000). *The Hengwrt Chaucer Digital Facsimile*. Leicester: Scholarly Digital Editions

7
Creating Learning Communities in Chaucer Studies: Process and Product

Gail Ashton

The Winter 2005 edition of *Arthuriana* is dedicated to a discussion of "teaching Arthuriana Materials." There, its guest editor, Maud Burnett McInerney, remarks the "fact that the demographics of courses on medieval literature have changed in interesting ways." Increasingly, as teachers we are faced with disparate cohorts of students—specialists and non-specialists, final year undergraduates/postgraduates and others, each with its own pressure regarding assessment and each arriving with conflicting expectations and demands (McInerney 2005: 4). With this in mind, an "Introduction to Middle English" course—more aptly termed a selection from Chaucer's *The Canterbury Tales*—that regularly recruits around 200 students becomes a potentially highly problematic gift.

The course in question occupied a unique place in Manchester University's now reinvigorated English and American literature programme. Its status as a first year course contributing only as a Pass/Fail marker of progression into the next year, and not towards final degree classification, is similar to other UK institutions. Yet it also functioned, not unusually, as a showcase for later medieval literature modules, raising questions about Chaucer's conflicted place in that spectrum that I do not intend to pursue here. In practice, its high recruitment figure tended to result from its favoured place in a "choose one of the following three" options where some were seeking actively to avoid one, or both, of the other course choices. Additionally, this option was repeated in Year II and was also available as a free choice for joint honours students, plus those from a variety of other disciplines. Its course title, a requisite of Faculty's branding of Year I course options, also tended to misdirect some, those Modern Languages or Erasmus/Exchange students attracted by an "English" that it never addressed.

My initial aim was pragmatic as well as pedagogical: to draw together this disparate student body and to provide the course with greater focus and cohesion. I assumed from the start that few arrived with any formal or lengthy familiarity with Chaucer Studies. So, my choice of texts began with *Sir Thopas* and ended with the *Knight's Tale*, taking in the Miller, The Wife of Bath, the Summoner, the Pardoner and the Merchant along the way. We read in Middle English but freely used modernisations. The course emphasised contemporary theoretical approaches and an awareness (through group project tasks, for example) of Chaucer as a living tradition.

But this essay is less about my commodified version of Chaucer than the ways in which this medieval author lends himself so readily to active, student-centred, project-based modes of teaching and learning. Feelings of alienation are common amongst students encountering university for the first time and are exacerbated by large class sizes in lecture halls or even in class: at that time, seminars regularly contained twenty or more students. A course unit that does not make explicit its aims or ethos merely compounds a sense that students somehow drift, more or less successfully, through university. In a conscious attempt to alleviate, in part, this problem and seek greater engagement from students, I use WebCT, my institution's computer software management system, to deliver my course unit. All of the course materials are posted on WebCT: course aims, assessment requirements, lecture and class times, lecture notes and handouts, a bibliography and webography, links to other on-line Chaucer resources, and, in this case, specific sections devoted to project work. I use two other WebCT resources: a planner to remind of events, post messages or add advice, and an electronic discussion board open to all students on the course, and with both a "reply privately" facility and private virtual spaces for smaller groups who wish to communicate with their own group project fellows.

At once, then, the design of the course cross-cuts its large number of registrants and communicates in a variety of ways. Non-compulsory lectures run approximately every other week; that same session the following week puts aside a set time for designated group meetings (to be supplemented as and how students decide) and/or consultation with tutors or the Course Director (me). Students meet at lectures, in class, and in their own self-selected groups for the group project I discuss later. They can access materials for the course 24-7 via WebCT which provides everything they need to know about this course. In this way, the dynamics of the seminar or classroom are taken outside to open up a virtual space that facilitates communication and direct student involvement, regardless of the constrictions of time or place.

My ethos for the course I describe can be summarised by the following key words: student-centred, collaboration, dialogue, community. I encourage accountable learning, in that I ask students to invest in and become responsible for what they do. This type of learning has implications for students and teachers alike, either of whom may be unfamiliar, even resistant, to its strategies and/or the tools used to implement it. A focus upon discussion and dialogue requires students to participate in an ongoing process of development. In turn, this promotes not only greater engagement, but a deeper understanding of what a course might bring. In such a dynamic, too, authority shifts away from the teacher who is no longer an expert but a facilitator, guiding students and providing opportunities for learning, rather than offering a master-class in which students passively digest content that is reproduced in certain, closed forms of assessment. How do we create learning communities of this kind, then, and why do I bring this to bear on Chaucer?

This single semester, 11 week module is assessed 50:50 between an individually graded portfolio (based on a group project) and a "seen" examination paper pre-released around Week 9. This allows opportunities for research and sharing of ideas and resources between students, but not tutors, prior to a traditional closed book exam. The group project similarly emphasises dialogue and collaborative working balanced by the portfolio which students work on alone. Assessment is, then, both summative, in the end product of exam, *and* formative, collaborative work in progress collated in the portfolio. This essay spotlights the group project/portfolio and the electronic discussion board, two aspects of the course that I think provide some productive possibilities and connections for Chaucer Studies. Both are medieval enterprises in spirit and in terms of their production. Both, too, offer us a large, unfinished process of reading, and interpretation, and writing, similar to the making of *The Canterbury Tales*. Also of interest is the unique dynamics of the discussion board, where audience participation actively shapes meaning, and texts—here messages or postings—may spin out of "authorial" control. The course, thus, opens up the issue of authority so central to Chaucer's works, here asking whose course/dialogue is it and how do we negotiate its peculiar textuality?

The group project

From the start students are asked to form groups, loosely defined as two plus, and agree on an investigation that involves all members in its processes. For the group project, they choose from one of the following:

A post-16/undergraduate study guide on ONE Chaucer tale of your choice.
Include a variety of material presented in a format and style suitable for your target audience.
OR
A creative response to a selection of Chaucer tales in any form (poetry, prose, drama script).
Please note: if you choose this option you will need to include a commentary explaining what choices you made/format used and why.
OR
You have been commissioned to produce material for a non-specialist or post-16/undergraduate audience on the theme of Chaucer in the Contemporary World. Your material may take any form (written, web pages, a radio or tv script, video or CD-ROM format . . .). What will you include and why?

Supporting advice is posted on WebCT alongside these options. It offers suggestions for starting points in terms of reading and research and also for the kinds of independent lines of inquiry students might pursue. The last option, for example, includes the production of an annotated anthology of favourite tales; critical appraisal of some Chaucer websites including consideration of the issue of translation or web projects like the Variorum Chaucer; discussion of Chaucer in popular culture (the "Canterbury Tales Experience" at Canterbury, the 2003 BBC1 TV adaptations, Chaucer at the Swan Theatre in Stratford, 2005/06); the Chaucer who appears on examination syllabi in schools and colleges; and so on.

The response to this aspect of the course is always overwhelmingly positive. This is evidenced by both the quality and, at times, the quantity of the work produced for the portfolios through which the project is assessed. Many students comment on the relative autonomy the project permits them and also on the benefits of working together towards an outcome with which they are more engaged than they might be if the tasks demanded were simply class exercises. However, some of the comments on student feedback forms from the first time I ran this course unit led to a rethink in terms of the requirements for this crucial part of the module.

Some complained about the need to replicate material for all members of the group when the portfolio is, after all, awarded an individual not group grade. Faculty requirements that students must submit two copies of all assessed work exacerbates this; someone in a group of four, for example, has, then, to copy their input eight times in total. Some course tutors also disliked handling weighty portfolios during the marking process. The question of length thus became a real issue. Though I had specified a word limit for the portfolio in keeping with what was usual for Year I students at my institution, I had also indicated that we would not penalise portfolios that ran over that, in my view, extremely short, 1500 word limit. More interested in process than product, I had not sufficiently considered the fact that students, especially first year, first semester undergraduates, are often primarily concerned only with final grades. The original course unit I designed asked students to include in their portfolio evidence of at least three specified criteria from a range published on WebCT. In practice, then, many portfolios were packed with often superfluous information. Some students felt pressured to "hit" their three specified target criteria and so, when in doubt, included more rather than less. Equally, with the word count relaxed, there was little incentive to edit or organise material with the result that those examining the portfolios sometimes found them overwhelming rather than illuminating to read.

These findings amply demonstrate that a student-centred style of teaching and learning demands that we structure our courses with especial care. My use of student survey forms builds in an opportunity for reflection from the start. As a result, it was soon clear that the requirements for assessment of the portfolio were needlessly complex, particularly given its unequal weighting—worth only thirty per cent of the final grade—in its trial run. All of this pandered to a culture of grade obsession that, in turn, aggravated the latent tendencies of brand new university students, fresh from a diet high in content and testing, to focus on end product rather than a formative, reflective process of learning. In addition, a free choice of topic for the project compounded the anxieties of new undergraduates who often arrive ill-equipped to manage a more independent, research-based mode of working.

Thus I modified the group project to place parameters upon choice. Now students select from three specified activities in line with the examples I gave earlier. Learning outcomes are also much clearer. Students must offer a portfolio: as evidence of research, complete with proper citations and accurate, formal referencing; and as evidence of reflection on the group project *as a whole*, as well as their individual contribution (to include, for example, ideas for further investigation and some thoughts on the processes and dynamics of devising and working through such a project as a group). In this way, I seek to raise awareness that this is a community of learning, not a model of lone scholarship. Equally, my choice of portfolio rather than an essay based on individual input into the project is a manoeuvre designed to make students reflect upon their learning as a constant, often open-ended or unfinished, *process*. The word count for individual contributions remains at 1500 words and is enforced in the same way as other coursework submitted to the department. This means that students must collate the portfolio according to an explicit organising principle.

Yet some profound implications remain. Students may fear that lack of commitment or participation by others in the group will adversely affect their own grades. This is especially pertinent to final year undergraduates in UK institutions where, typically, every piece of work contributes towards a final degree classification, or else in the US where graduates work alongside those who are assessed at a different level. My experience is that, in practice, students exhibit less concern about the effects of drop-out, illness or sheer laziness than we might anticipate once they are familiar with the styles of engagement and learning these sorts of courses demand. By emphasising process, no one in a given group is penalised by the failure of others, for whatever reasons, to submit their piece or for the group's inability to complete the overall project. Equally, if a particular line of enquiry proves less fruitful than anticipated, as long as alternatives are suggested and the portfolio offers evidence of reflection on its processes, then risks are minimised.

Central to the pedagogical practices that structure my course is the commitment to a philosophy of collaborative learning that is itself suggestive of ways of dealing with people which respects and highlights individual group members' abilities and contributions. Ted Panitz (1996) describes the resultant sharing of authority and acceptance of responsibility among group members for the group's actions. Both the group project and the (optional) electronic discussion board are integral elements of a course unit that is concerned with co-operation and consensus building, through the sharing of ideas and research findings. Even though the group project is assessed by individual grade, my insistence on reflection upon the processes and practices of the *group's* research aims, as well as individual contributions, deconstructs what Panitz (1996) calls the impetus of "competition in which individuals best the other group members." Thus the student who works independently of his/her group has an in-built ceiling on their grade.

My use of the term collaborative learning is judiciously chosen. Panitz's on-line discussion paper (1996) identifies it as student-centred activity in which process, sharing and discovery (as the activities worked out through discussion) are crucial. Students work relatively autonomously, forming groups on the basis of friendship and/or interest without teacher intervention or direct supervision. Gokhale (1995) describes how, in contrast, co-operative learning retains stronger teacher controls and is quantitative in ethos, concerned with achievement and assessment, with the *product* of learning, gained *incidentally* by interacting in order to reach a particular goal. Research suggests that a course designed on the basis of collaborative principles encourages an active exchange of ideas that, in turn, enhances central thinking skills. Students are better equipped to analyse, synthesise and evaluate materials, texts and issues they work with. They are required to make cross-connections and conscious choices about which line of inquiry or research to pursue in an enterprise that makes them take responsibility, not only for their own learning, but, for that of others in the group too (Johnson and Johnson 2000; Gokhale 1995).

Students self-select their groups; they organise these according to their own criteria and meet outside the classroom. Advice published on WebCT reminds them of some of the implications of these choices (how friendship groups sometimes encourage sympathetic consensus rather than open dialogue) and suggests ways in which they might keep track of their investigations or ensure everyone has an active role to play. Some needed guidance on how to think more flexibly about a project. A creative writing choice still demands careful research and an awareness, perhaps, of how medieval textual production differs from our own; not everyone needs to be a creative genius in order to participate in that option. In this way, students begin to reflect upon how they work and learn together. Ideally, teacher-input into these processes will be supportive rather than overt. Even the advisory materials published on WebCT might be produced by former students of the course, thereby enabling further investment in future learning communities.

In practice, these strategies are also stressful for teachers and students alike, especially when they remain out of step with a more traditional, competitive ethos of learning. The first time my own course ran, two teachers attempted to allocate students to groups, despite my intentions. Students were quick to respond to a perceived inequity, complaining about the lack of constraint enjoyed by their peers. A few also asked to work alone rather than in a group. Many demanded more lectures at the expense of designated group meeting time. One even complained that course delivery through WebCT was teaching "on the cheap". Equally, many students continue to obsess about grades. What is at stake here is a focus on product that reflects and, in turn, indicts a culture of competition reified by constant testing and publication of results. Panitz (1996) indicates that students are unlikely to embrace collaborative learning unless they are exposed to it early on and trained in its methods. Nico Wiersema's on-line discussion paper (2000) concurs. He comments that if teachers do not continually reinforce the philosophy of process, students will seek strategies that circumvent it by returning them to more familiar styles of learning "and only do whatever they can do to get a good grade."

Clearly the context of a course is crucial. Complaints and concerns of the type I have just described lessened considerably on the second course. There, learning outcomes were more carefully thought out but, above all, its place in the department's curriculum was different. On this occasion it was not a stand-alone first year unit. Instead, it ran concurrently with compulsory core modules also delivered through WebCT. Students were more familiar with its style which was perceived as in-house rather than idiosyncratic or experimental. Collaborative learning works best when everyone, including teachers, buy-in to its ethos. That ethos needs to be transparent and its practical implications thought out if we are to emphasise what Wiersema calls "positive interdependence" (Wiersema 2000). Those with the most recent and, by implication, successful experience of traditional "bite-sized" top-down courses, aimed at steering students through public examinations in our schools and colleges, are paradoxically the most open and, yet, most resistant to attempts to promote independent learning.

Even the most apparently unstructured courses retain at their heart the authority of their designers. However open the course I construct, of necessity it still imposes a particular ethos and teaching/learning style upon its takers. It insists too upon delivery through an electronic medium. Those who sign up for the course must also register with and actively use WebCT if they are to access any course materials: from class and lecture times and places, to its week by week structure. Those who miss a class for any reason can always find the topic for the next class in advance. In short, those who choose this course become accountable for their own learning right from the start. This means that each element they choose to ignore has consequences. No one is compelled to use the discussion board; those who do gain access to discussion, shared resources and strands of potential research as well as evidence for their portfolio. Attendance at lectures is not compulsory; without it, any handouts downloaded from WebCT are next to useless and it becomes more difficult to access the discussions that erupt on the board. Other facilities, such as timed release of lecture notes, virtual classes, or phased release of additional, supporting material (which could then be withdrawn) pull individuals into a community of learners.

Students quickly recognise these covert pressures and respond positively. But, sometimes, it is hard for teachers to realise that their behaviour also needs to change if students are to become accountable. Those who select groups for students encourage that group to abdicate responsibility for its own learning. Each time we print off material for an unresponsive class instead of sending them to the resources bank on WebCT, or reply (as I did) to e-mails requesting information that is already posted, we reinforce passive modes of learning. Of course, there is a balance to be drawn. Many students lack the skills and resources necessary to cope with unfamiliar modes of teaching and learning. As such, they need training in their use (I have a compulsory lecture on using WebCT at the start of the course) and, opportunity for consultation. My point is that we are often guilty of failing to relinquish our control as teachers; in so doing, we undermine our own attempts to instil good practice in our students.

Equally, as Simons and Maidment (2004) indicate, there are heavy costs involved when setting up courses of this type: in terms of planning, design and initial tutor support. I was fortunate enough to have funding from Distributed Learning in the first instance which bought me out of teaching, gave me a Learning Practitioner who offered hands-on support throughout, and also a postgraduate peer mentor. Once the course has been modified, though, it begins to run itself, especially if its management, and consequently ownership, is transferred to students. IT support is also an issue. For teachers, it is crucial and must be in place throughout. Neither should we dismiss those students who resist such courses on the grounds that they lack easy access to a PC or are concerned about viruses or computer failure. Though this stems from a goal-oriented approach and neglects the value of transferable IT skills, it is important that we address it as a genuine concern from the start by offering training sessions and advertising technological support.

Feedback and implications

It is always tempting to brush aside adverse criticism of a course's design, especially those that are isolated examples. Yet it is precisely there that our attention as reflective practitioners ought to rest. In some respects, the more open, and, hence, successful, learning communities we create, the more susceptible to dissent we become. Here we are returned to those questions of control and authority that lurk at the edges of this essay. With this in mind, I would like to turn my attention to both student survey returns and to those comments circulating in the public domain on the discussion board.

I have already indicated that those students currently opting for this course see nothing remarkable about the manner in which it is facilitated, not least because it is one of several such courses running at first year level (and beyond). There remain, however, significant differences in terms of vision and, in particular, management of the discussion boards that these courses incorporate. This became apparent in a spontaneous and exceptionally long thread on my own board when students sparked a controversy that catapulted us all into a wider pedagogical debate. Students in this particular cohort used my discussion board voluntarily as part of the processes of learning I have already described. In contrast, the discussions on the core course that ran concurrently with mine utilised a "push" principle and stressed the production of measurable learning outcomes. As such, students participated in a compulsory e-learning forum. The 200-plus students on that course were subdivided into virtual classes, matching their real-life class, with both quantity and quality of their postings in this forum assessed. Our diametrically opposed philosophies clashed in a remarkable demonstration of the empowerment students experience when allowed to open up their own dialogues. In this thread, many accused the "rival" board of promoting rehearsed debates, "formulated observations and mini-essays." Most claimed that they posted simply to hit the target of twenty indicated in the published criteria for assessment. Others complained that such a restricted dialogue stifled genuine debate. My own board received a thumbs-up, but, perhaps more significantly, this dialogue suggests that students are acutely conscious of the centrality of discussion in literature and of the need to allow it to develop without too many constraints, something for another discussion paper altogether.

Yet for every student who posts on my open-style discussion board, there are three, even four, who do not. This active refusal to participate works against my ideas of collaboration and dialogue and, as such, it is interesting to consider the implications of this choice. Student survey returns indicate that most of these non-contributors are "lurkers," that is those who read, and presumably think about what they read, but do not reply. This passive consumption of the ideas of others is an issue in any class or seminar, and clearly anathema to notions of active learning, but the situation is far more complex than it appears. Some indicated that they did not actively post because "everyone else seems so clever."

Certainly, some contributions may have the effect of intimidating others. There is enough superficial similarity between on-line messages and the verbal comments of real-life contexts to make this an issue for some, though discouraging lengthy "composed" replies, through, for example, non-compulsory boards and by adopting an informal tone in our own questions and messages, goes some small way towards alleviating this. In part, the high status that we award the written word is also a contributory factor. Even on a free board, some students retain a fearful sense of the hidden "I" of its designer (all too often a teacher) and so, again, refuse to participate. Many of these add that they do use boards or virtual spaces of this type outside university curricula indicating an awareness that the board is not, after all, owned by them but by the controlling forces of the academic institution in which they work.

This awareness of surveillance in the discussions that take place, even on boards that profess none, is an issue. I find that students often refer to me in their postings, either indirectly or, more often, by name. In part this is affirmative; many are humorous asides that include me within the community the board constructs: "Aw, Gail's reduced to pleading . . . bless!" Someone else hoped that I'd enjoy the parodic poem he had posted, the "Chaucer Pubbe Gagge." Another advised her peers against reading a particular critic concluding with "sorry if you like her Gail." What these examples suggest is that even open dialogue carries a prevailing ethos that takes its tenor from those who seemingly own it. No other tutors were mentioned, directly or otherwise. From this, I infer that in signing myself as Course Director and delivering the lecture programme myself, I somehow publicly asserted an ownership I said I did not possess (or that students invested in me an authority I also claimed I had abdicated).

A further example of this is the extended dialogue that occurred in response to a lecture in which I had "queered" the figure of the Pardoner. Increasingly, one student found himself defending a lonely position on the board. His response turned the attack on the closed ethos of a prevailing dialogue that overwhelmingly affirmed the critical approach I had taken: "To Gail, you did say be honest and I was . . . to everyone else, if you disagree with me, good! It's getting a bit tedious reading the same sycophantic messages every day." Later, the same student observed that perhaps I had consciously set out to provoke controversy and added, "Well done Gail, it worked!" These responses illustrate that collaboration also has collusion as its implicit "other." Communal dialogue creates its own borders, and, by definition, its exclusions. Those made uncomfortable by its prevailing style, those fearing exposure, or those unable to find a point at which to enter opt out, or lurk.

My experiences in this respect corroborate other pedagogical research which points out that "the specialized nature of [the] discussion groups can become too insular and force out dissenting voices" (Smith & Kollock 1999: 20 and 259). I suggest, too, that discussion board use has relatively low social costs for its contributors and, as such, implicitly invites this tension between open, unrestricted dialogue (with the subsequent transfer of control and ownership to students) *and* acute awareness of covert surveillance mechanisms. All postings carry a name and/or a student ID number; their responses can be archived and traced. Yet virtual messaging also has a disinhibiting effect; though patently public, the space offers the illusion of privacy. All messages carry a name, but not everyone knows to whom these names belong and, without any face-to-face interaction, users may create identities or personas for themselves. This seems somehow apposite for a Chaucer course, as does the way in which the board is organised, via loosely thematic threads that do not correspond to a completed, whole "story." Instead, contributors begin to construct a communal dialogue *for themselves*.

In this way, too, lurking becomes a positive response as well as an undesirable. Those who regularly read the board but do not actively post are still complicit in its operations. The peculiar dynamics of this virtual space mean that each act of reading is also an act of interpretation. Readers work through the threads that the board visibly produces for them. They may enter a debate at a moment of their choosing to read all or part of it, to read retrospectively or prospectively, to read threads within threads or not as they wish. They are, then, compelled to make conscious decisions and connections in order to construct meaning rather than reading passively by simply following a linear progression of ideas. The board is written, too, not by me or by anyone with any critical or academic standing, but by students who can edit or annotate other messages, quoting them in full, for example, or in part, to shift emphasis or subtly alter meaning or status. The asynchronicity (time lag between postings) of these boards further ensures that its "talk" can never be purely linear, while the fluidity of its parameters lets discussion move in any direction.

It is precisely those layers of interaction within any virtual community that leave me less concerned abut those who lurk than I might be in a real classroom. The discussion board conversations are simply not the same as conventional verbal interactions. Neither does their dynamic resemble the usual reading-writing model that comes into play when we read conventional texts. In many ways, the interplay of audience-reader-author, where the status of author is ambivalent, more closely models that of medieval textuality, an interesting bonus for those of us teaching literature of that period. Forced to make connections in and between threads, readers and writers of discussion boards quickly learn that meaning is often more subtle, contingent and variable than we remember.

Of course, open dialogue leaves plenty of room for challenges. I suggest that far from viewing this as negative, it in fact indicates that the board is achieving its aim of promoting student investment in learning, an idea corroborated by Kirkpatrick's study of on-line "chat" in virtual classrooms (2005). As students begin to invest in a course, its designer is sometimes called to account in ways I have already described. More than once, students have commented on a perceived bias in my own teaching that neglects, in their opinion, explicit social commentary on the medieval world. One objected to a canonical writer like Chaucer being "reduced to a medieval Benny Hill." To my surprise, this comment was greeted with an outpouring of protest perhaps best summarised by the following reply: "call me naïve but surely one of the biggest cruxes of social context is gender and sexuality . . . Shakespeare writing girls for boys playing girls dressed as men anyone?" In this instance, an attack upon a course's values opens into a broader discussion of theoretical approaches and concerns in direct contradiction of one student's belief that virtual dialogues are never "dynamic or spontaneous like it is in seminars . . . qualities which by its very nature WebCT cannot possess."

Community

Throughout this essay, I have emphasised that what is at stake in an enterprise of this kind is a sense of a learning community. As evidence, examples of mutual support and sharing abound on the discussion boards I have used. The apologetic concern of the student posting the "Chaucer Pubbe Gagge," that it is too facile for such a course, receives affirmation in "Wish I could write poetry like that, even if it was only a parody of a greater work! Thanks for sharing!" Another student asks if anyone has found a better tale than the Summoner's, is forced by others to define "better" and then wonders "what does everyone else think? . . . am I looking at it too superficially?" There are numerous instances of students thanking each other for sharing views and ideas, of spontaneous advice on translating or reading Chaucer in Middle English (clearly a concern), or of visible models of helping as they share resources and research. Ideally, I would hope to see students making thoughtful connections between and across course units or recognising that some of the issues we have explored impact on popular culture and take Chaucer out into a living tradition of texts and ideas. Some did exactly this with postings about the intersections of primary texts and the 2003 BBC1 television adaptations of some of the *Tales*. Others explored how Chaucer's intervention in the genre of heroic romance, through *Sir Thopas*, was similar to ideas garnered from another course unit's lecture on "Masterplots." Someone else compared the idea of "queering" famous texts to "slash" on the Internet. Others thought the "touch of the queer" had overlap with the ideas of 1970s musicians like Bowie and Bryan Ferry of *Roxy Music*.

Postscript

One of the major implications of this type of student-centred learning is that it demands commitment to its philosophy and appreciation of the ambivalent dynamics it introduces. Its shift away from closed master–student scenarios to the creation of learning communities, in which dialogue is crucial and where students become accountable for their own learning, is not always easy to negotiate. At the same time, its context in a wider course provision needs to be addressed if its ethos and practices are not to be viewed as merely experimental. When this course came up for review, it was moved into Year II of our undergraduate programme and its group project options revised accordingly. During my prolonged absence from the university, that entire programme was refreshed and its assessment homogenised. The course disappeared and seems unlikely to return.

Works cited

Gokhale, Anuradha A. (1995). *Collaborative Learning Enhances Critical Thinking* http://scholar.lib.vt.edu/ejournals/JTE/jte-v7n1/gokhale.jte-v7n1.html

Johnson, D. W. & F. P. Johnson (2000). *Joining Together: Group Theory and Group Skills*. Boston, MA: Allyn and Bacon

Kirkpatrick, Graeme (2005). "Online 'Chat' Facilities as Pedagogic Tools: A Case Study," *Active Learning in Higher Education*, 6.2: 145–59

McInerney, Maud Burnett (2005). "Introduction", *Arthuriana*, 15: 1–5

Panitz, Ted (1996). *A Definition of Collaborative vs Cooperative Learning*
http://www. city.londonmet.ac.uk/deliberations/collaborativelearning/
panitz2.html

Simons, John & Brian Maidment (2004). "The Origins of the Reading Public,
1830–70", *English Subject Centre Newsletter*, 6: 25–7

Smith, Marc A. & Peter Kollock, ed. (1999). *Communities in Cyberspace.* New York
and London: Routledge

Wiersema, Nico (2000). *How Does Collaborative Learning Actually Work in a
Classroom and How Do Students React to It? A Brief Reflection*
http://www.city.londonmet.ac.uk/deliberations/collaborativelearning/wiersem
a.html

8

"The wondres that they myghte seen or heere": Designing and Using Web-based Resources to Teach Medieval Literature

Philippa Semper

The wealth of material now available in electronic form includes a vast range of resources on medieval literature. The "world of Chaucer," so ably presented in traditional printed form by Derek Brewer (2000) can now be usefully supplemented by the "World Wide Web on Chaucer," while a large corpus of other important Middle English texts have also appeared with attendant background and critical commentary (for a review of useful sites and discussion of possibilities and pitfalls, see Semper 2005: 607–19). As a result, those who teach medieval texts, including Chaucer and his literary and linguistic contexts, face the challenge of making this web-based material not only accessible but also meaningful to students. Having texts, images and sounds readily available removes many of the traditional restrictions on course design, and also promises to allow students to tailor their studies and pursue their individual interests as independent learners. On the other hand, there is a real possibility that the quality of course delivery is compromised if there is no correlation between the kinds of material students access on the Web and those which they encounter in more traditional teaching and learning scenarios: the lecture hall, or the seminar room, or the library. What follows is an account of the ways in which some of the possibilities of web-based learning were put into practice in modules on Chaucer and medieval literature in my own Department, including the issues encountered and the lessons learnt.

Issues

When creating e-resources for teaching medieval literature and in putting them into use, there are several issues that must be considered. As new generations of students arrive at university accustomed to surfing the Web, the types of course provision and academic training relevant to their needs and experience change. It is now only rarely the case that technology forms a barrier between students and their electronic resources: few college or university entrants need to be taught what the Web is or how to get access to it. However, this brings new challenges. Many students now surf the Web as a first, rather than last, resort when faced with researching an essay; yet they need to be taught to discriminate between resources, and to understand the standards of content appropriate for study in higher education. Hence, when students are approaching a new subject area, electronic resources are generally most effective when used in very specific contexts: guidance towards particular webpages or sites, focused discussion as to their content, and requirements for defined levels of usage can train students in what to look for and what to assess in the kinds of material encountered on the Web. As a JISC project investigating the design and use of e-learning interventions in learning discovered, "it is the *use* in context of interventions that is important" (Littlejohn 2004: 10–11).

The extent of student–tutor interaction necessary for "effective intervention" in relation to e-learning remains debatable, of course. Should *every* kind of electronic resource be directly combined with tutor-moderated activities in order to ensure effectiveness and aid the development of active learning styles? In what respects can this be said to be both pedagogically beneficial *and* cost-effective? (See, for example, Fox & MacKeogh 2003: 121–34.) This is a contentious issue: in a recent paper, the authors quoted as a view given in discussion that "to suggest that people can't learn without human interaction would suggest that people can't learn anything by reading a book in the quiet of a library" (O'Neill, Singh & O'Donoghue 2004: 317). Yet this apparently pithy response is both limited and limiting. Teachers are increasingly aware that many of their students apparently *can't* learn anything in this way; used to almost constant background noise, and not necessarily equipped with functional note-taking skills, some students find the silence of the library oppressive and the concentration they need elusive.

Learning styles are not homogenous when it comes to e-learning, any more than they are in traditional seminar or lecture room (or library) situations. Different students require access to learning materials to be facilitated in different ways, with more or less human interaction according to their levels and habitual practices. Sweeping statements on either side of the debate will not help us to create and deploy effective learning resources or environments. As Mayes and de Freitas point out, "there are really no models of e-learning *per se*—only e-enhancements of models of learning . . . using technology to achieve better learning outcomes, or a more effective assessment of these outcomes, or a more cost-efficient way of bringing the learning environment to the learners" (Mayes & de Freitas).

Such a view of the use of electronic resources in specific contexts, but in a way that leads to improved learning outcomes, underlies my own experience of using the Web to teach Chaucer. Consideration of these issues drove the provision we made to support modules on Middle English texts in general, and Chaucer in particular, at the University of Birmingham from 2000 to 2005.

Design

My own arrival at Birmingham in September of 2000 coincided with the initiation of electronic resources into the support of core modules in the medieval sector of the English Department. From the beginning, my role was to turn the idea into a reality. This offered its own challenges, not least in relation to the variety and flexibility required for our e-resources to respond to both student and staff needs. For, while various members of staff in the Department had individual webpages which supported their own teaching and research interests, provision for a core module in the Department had to be answerable to the teaching of several different members of staff and also to postgraduate teaching assistants. The staffing level was high because large student numbers were involved; every student had to take one of the core medieval modules in either their second or third year. Not only did the provision need to be robust, but it had to be sufficiently flexible to answer to the varying learning styles and knowledge bases of students at two levels of study.

The first core module to be supported was "Authorising English: Power and Textual Practice," designed by Wendy Scase. This began with the study of Chaucer in the final years of the fourteenth century and continued through to 1560, covering authors in the Chaucerian tradition such as Lydgate and Hoccleve, and also Henryson and Dunbar. The module description invited students to consider "the idea of 'English literature' and of English literary 'authors'. . . seen under construction in this period" and enabled them to "investigate writing and textual practice in the period in relation to the cultural and social processes that generated these still-powerful categories of literary analysis." There was a strong emphasis on reading texts in the original language. Learning outcomes were also wide-ranging, including students' ability to "demonstrate breadth of reading in the writing of the period and knowledge of the work of at least four authors, named or anonymous; demonstrate breadth of research, showing knowledge, where appropriate, of the ideas, institutions, events and processes that shaped or were shaped by literary production and textual culture in the period; demonstrate reflective awareness of possible critical positions, showing knowledge . . . of modern critical discussion and debate; show knowledge of the characteristic literary styles, genres and discourses of the period." The description and outcomes made explicit the requirements for on-line provision; it would have to support both the students' interactions with Middle English language, and their acquisition of sufficient background knowledge to support their explorations of texts in several contexts and from various critical perspectives.

The module alternated on a yearly basis with "Reinventing English: Vernacular Textualities," which began by looking at texts from the thirteenth century and moved towards a study of Chaucer at the end of the fourteenth century. While its learning outcomes were similar to those of "Authorising English," it focused upon the "imaginative, formal and thematic freedom . . . enabled by historically-specific, and shifting, configurations of language and literate culture" and allowed students to study "selected texts and authors of the later fourteenth century alongside earlier texts that experiment with vernacular literacy such as prose writings for women, and romance and lyric poetry." It shared an emphasis on reading in the original Middle English, and on the ability of students "to relate their analyses of specific texts to cultural circumstances and changes."

Both modules were delivered by means of two lecture hours and one seminar group a week. All students went to the same lectures, but attended either intermediate or higher level seminar groups so that the differences in learning outcomes and assessment between the levels could be sensibly addressed by tutors. They were assessed by means of a three-hour examination paper, which required them to bring their knowledge of the literature to bear upon unseen essay questions. At intermediate level, this involved answering three questions: two answers had to contain detailed analysis of a single text, while the third answer examined at least two separate texts. Overall, candidates had to show that they knew the work of at least three authors; for most this meant in practice that they discussed Chaucer and two others. At higher level this involved answering only two questions, but since the time allotted remained the same, the answers were expected to address the questions in considerably more detail. Overall, the work of at least four authors had to be discussed, which meant that students analysed a minimum of two texts and authors per answer; usually this would work out as Chaucer and three other authors.

Given that "Authorising English" would be taught from the beginning of October 2000, the time-scale was tight, and a combination of past experience and good advice from others was essential. I had been using a Virtual Learning Environment (VLE) called TopClass to teach *Beowulf* at University College Dublin since 1998, but TopClass was not available at Birmingham. The chosen VLE, WebCT, had not yet been rolled out throughout the University. As a result, there was not sufficient infrastructure in place to register and initiate a large group of students into its use at very short notice in the second or final year of their degree, so using a VLE did not seem like a sensible choice, either practically or pedagogically.

The alternative was to provide a specific website for the module, which acted as both a repository and a portal. This allowed us to consider a model that would answer to our administrative needs in relation to the overall delivery of the module, as well as giving us the flexibility both to create our own content and to direct students towards pre-existing resources that would be useful to them. A further element of the model was its accessibility: the resource was neither password-protected nor site-specific, making it available to staff and students wherever they happened to be. The use of the website was designed to augment traditional teaching sessions, rather than to replace them; however, it also allowed more variety of activity and range of material in these too, since preparation using electronic resources before sessions could be integrated into face-to-face discussions and small-group work.

This model represented a form of "blended learning" (also sometimes referred to as "hybrid learning"), although its aim was not to produce an interactive environment combining electronic resources with on-line tasks. Rather, it brought together a "mix of different media" (Koper 2001), combining library resources and information about module delivery with pre-existing subject-specific webpages and some resources that we ourselves created for the site. A recent article has claimed that "significant differences exist among the various formats and . . . the internet-based format could possibly lead to better student outcomes compared to face-to-face and hybrid formats" (Reasons, Valadares and Slavkin 2005). However, we found blended learning to be a useful way of training students to interact with and evaluate e-resources, *without* placing all the emphasis upon on-line activity at an early stage in their introduction to an unfamiliar area of study. When dealing with a subject which some students claimed to find taxing, given its requirement that they engage with medieval English language, literature, culture and history, the combination of traditional face-to-face seminar discussion with extensive use of e-resources made sense. Effectively, the web pages allowed teachers to concentrate on areas of difficulty or interest during seminars and lectures, while directing students towards the site for extra "information" (such as historical data) and for "self-help" tools (such as Middle English language pages).

So useful was this model that I used it again when creating web-based support for a specialist, higher-level module in Chaucer, ("Pre-Modern Writing, Post-Modern Readings") taught by Wendy Scase. Its final incarnation was in response to our curriculum change, when "Authorising English" and "Reinventing English" were both replaced by a single, intermediate-level module dealing with material from 1380 to 1560, called "Writing Society."

Content

With this model of provision, the challenge was to provide a resource that answered to the learning outcomes of the module *and* was more than just "a content repository" with "limited active learner participation" (O'Neill, Singh & O'Donoghue 2004: 313). Since we were not using a VLE, the structure of the site needed to encourage active learning, but yet at the same time it was important that "the format should not obscure the content but help to facilitate it" (Manning, Cohen, & DeMichiell 2003: 119). In practice, this resulted in a mixture of content types organised in various ways in order to respond to the interests of the module and a range of learning styles.

The first stage, then, was to decide what was needed and how best to provide it. The various areas could be roughly listed as follows:

- Middle English language (including pronunciation guides, grammar, glossaries and dictionaries)
- primary texts and authors (including electronic texts and biographical information)
- key words and concepts

- historical context and background (including timelines and archaeology)
- secondary literature
- information on resources in Birmingham and the West Midlands
- module information (including reading list, lecture schedule, assessment details and so on).

It rapidly became clear that some of this could be provided by setting up focused subject "portals" which allowed students to access electronic resources already on the Web. This proved most useful for the Middle English language material; a page with annotated hyperlinks directed students to sites where, for example, they could listen to Middle English read aloud, find explanations of spelling conventions and the Great Vowel Shift, and consult the *Middle English Dictionary* on-line (see, for example, the Harvard Chaucer pages, *The Great Vowel Shift* and the *Middle English Dictionary* websites). We were able to point students towards the language resources as part of their module preparation material before teaching started, enabling the more diligent and enthusiastic to get ahead with reading primary texts and improving their language skills.

However, if the content was to be kept flexible and the site easy to use, portals for every text or author or idea did not seem to be the answer. Instead, we found two ways of grouping information. The first was by creating the "Key Words and Concepts" resource for the module, which was a type of greatly extended glossary. Wendy Scase and David Griffith wrote short pieces to explain words and concepts from an agreed list; these included entries from "Catholics and Protestants" and "Chivalry" through to "Vernacular" and "Wyclif." Each entry was then linked and cross-referenced on-line, and accessed through an index page. The entries were used to provide focused reading and resources: each entry contained an explanation of the term, a short bibliography containing further reading and, if appropriate, hyperlinks to other material on the Web. For example, the entry for Lollardy included within its explanation links to entries on heresy, orthodoxy, John Wyclif, and saints' lives, and provided both a page of further links to "useful websites" and a selected bibliography (see Figure 8.1).

The "Key Words and Concepts" list became an adaptable learning object. As Koper explains, "a learning object can stand on its own and may be reused. In practice this means that learning objects are mostly smaller objects—smaller than courses—which can be reused in different courses" (Koper 2001). Our list was extremely valuable to us in relation

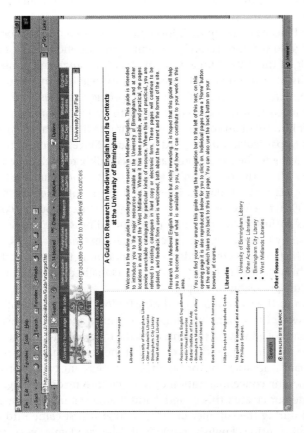

Figure 8.1 The entry for Lollardy from the "Key Words and Concepts" list. Reproduced by permission of the University of Birmingham.

to all the modules for which we used this model; we could incorporate the list as it was, add new entries if required, or remove entries that were not specifically relevant to a module. It was also an important element in building up the students' understanding of the people, ideas, texts and contexts of the later medieval period; the cross-referencing system ensured that students selected their own pathways through the information, and were more actively involved in making connections and grounding ideas within networks of information that they could tailor to their own needs and interests.

The second means of grouping information was based on the module structure; it followed the lecture programme for the module. In each case, the title of the lecture linked to a précis of its range and content, and also a list of suggested and supplementary reading and websites where appropriate. This means of providing specific resources according to pre-announced lectures enabled students to prepare thoroughly for lectures, to follow them up comprehensively, and to find with ease material relevant to particular authors, texts or issues. Since several lecturers were contributing to the lecture programme according to their expertise, this also gave them the opportunity to effectively "communicate" the focus of their lecture to students with whom they might otherwise have no contact, either before or after the delivery. Lecture resources could include links to further portals, of course, including sites such as the Harvard Geoffrey Chaucer website, the Luminarium Chaucer pages, and the Chaucer Metapage, giving students the opportunity to carry out their own research more widely or with a more personalised approach than generic module provision can supply.

In addition to the usual module administration, providing details of assessment, essay titles, sample examination papers and so on, we also wanted a means of educating students as to the range of on-line and off-line resources available at a local level, so that they could make the most of Birmingham's libraries, historical sites and museum collections as part of a widening conceptualisation of research into medieval English. I either located or created this material and then assembled the results into a guide during the summer of 2001, so that it first came into use with the Reinventing English module in the academic year that followed (see Figure 8.2). The Guide gave details as to local academic libraries, the City Library and other West Midlands libraries that students might find useful. It also supplied specially-produced lists of medieval-related books and slides available in the English Department (such as those in the Geoffrey Shepherd Library), and of medieval images and objects in the Barber Institute and the Birmingham Museum

129

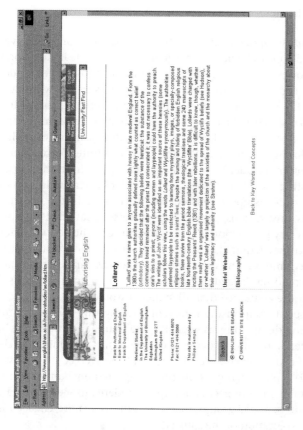

Figure 8.2 The "Guide to Research". Reproduced by permission of the University of Birmingham.

and Gallery. Finally, it included a series of pages detailing local sites of interest—medieval castles, manor houses, churches and so on. Thus it facilitated integrated access to several sources of information through which students could build their own structures of knowledge and form individual contexts for understanding the period, while making maximum use of specific resources available in Birmingham and the West Midlands.

Use in teaching

While students were free to explore the Web resources for themselves, a more directed approach could be particularly useful in teaching. For me, this worked on several levels. At its simplest, the Web enabled students to obtain a basic introduction to the period and its events without taking up valuable lecture time. Detailed timelines, brief historical introductions and even virtual reconstructions of medieval buildings were all available, in addition to a large and increasing quantity of digitised manuscript folios, providing a rich and almost infinitely extendable set of information that students could adapt and explore in relation to their own pre-existing knowledge-base and the kinds of texts and images they had decided to focus upon. This enabled them to gain the knowledge "of the ideas, institutions, events and processes that shaped or were shaped by literary production and textual culture in the period" that the module outcomes required. For tutors it meant that events (battles, plagues, riots, and so on) or characters (such as kings, archbishops, noblemen) could be flagged as important to the following week's discussion with the assurance that all students would be able to find out something about them in the intervening study time. More informed and interesting discussion was generally the result, and could also help to calm students' nerves; anxieties about their initially limited levels of period-specific knowledge were common but the Web could be systematically used to plug such gaps. At times, repeated encounters of references to certain issues or events prompted students to seek clarification about them in seminar groups, again leading to a more engaged and student-led exploration of the subject.

Obviously, use of the Web also widened the range of texts that could easily be read and analysed by all students beyond what was available in the prescribed anthology (we used Pearsall 1999 as our module anthology). It was therefore possible to ask a group to go and read another text on-line, and then return with their analysis of it in comparison to an anthology text that had been lectured upon that week. In a world of decreasing budgets for library acquisitions and increasing student numbers, this was a welcome alternative to making multiple copies of a single text available for very limited loan periods.[1] It equipped students with knowledge of a wider range of texts for their final assessment, but also broadened their understanding of the literary contexts in which all these texts could be understood. Guided exploration of a topic, person or idea was also possible using the site; for example, preparation for a seminar on *The Wife of Bath's Tale* could include consulting the "Key words and phrases list" for an introduction to and resources on medieval romance or on chivalry, as well as reading other Middle English versions of the Wife's tale on-line, such as *The Wedding of Sir Gawain and Dame Ragnell*. Access to the *Middle English Dictionary* through the Web meant that I could ask students to look up important words and come back with both a definition of their meaning and a knowledge of the other literary contexts in which they had been used, opening up the way for deeper and more informed analysis. Since some students were a little overwhelmed by the period, giving them delimited tasks to do or particular problems to solve created learning pathways for them, helped them to focus, and also gave them the satisfaction of learner involvement in the module.

An unexpected bonus was that consultation of websites in some instances seemed to improve student awareness of the importance of developing keen presentation skills. Having strained their eyes reading unpleasantly coloured texts against murky backgrounds, or become frustrated trying to find references on less scholarly webpages during surfing, they had a greater understanding of the issues involved for the reader when confronting text in other contexts than traditional, printed books and journals. Pedagogically, this brought opportunities for emphasising the necessity for scholarly attitudes to citation and documentation, and for encouraging the development of presentation skills, important for a graduate's *curriculum vitae* and transferable into most workplaces at some level.

Evaluation

Apart from ongoing feedback in seminars, we gathered student response to the website through module evaluation. This was done by means of an anonymous questionnaire at the end of each module, which asked students to assess the organisation, teaching, content and resources of the module, as well as their own performance. From this it became clear that there were certain aspects of our model that were widely appreciated, while others depended on the learning styles and personal circumstances of the students concerned. Overall, there was a very positive response to the organised and integrated nature of the modules as expressed through the website. This led in turn to approval of the design and organisation of the modules themselves: "best module so far in terms of planning" enthused one tutee. Students were particularly appreciative of the ways in which the model brought together and made explicit the themes and content of the module. As a final-year student put it, "I felt the module dealt very cohesively with the central themes . . . the information and materials on the website helped a lot in this respect." A further benefit came from providing the lecture programme and the précis and resources for each lecture; this enabled staff, as well as students, to see how others were dealing with the module content, and resulted in more coherent lecture–seminar relationships. The enthusiasm for this was clear from the student evaluation: "the lectures and seminars matched up! It was great!" said one, while another remarked that "it's good when lectures and seminars correspond."

In terms of content, certain areas were explicitly acknowledged, while others silently passed over. "The website was excellent in helping with the language," reported a student who had reported difficulties in reading Middle English elsewhere on the form. The language sites we linked to seemed popular, while there was less obvious take-up for secondary criticism on-line; students still seemed to prefer getting books from the Library to reading from the screen of their PC. References to the electronic resources available were often general, such as this comment: "I found the website content particularly useful . . . there were huge resources for this course on the Internet." However, the simple availability of this material by means of the website was particularly appreciated as students commented, "it was very easy to access the Internet (great website)."

This was interesting to correlate with general responses to the modules. As core provision, our modules were delivered to students ranging from the willing and able to the entirely unwilling who were not convinced that they were able to cope with this material. Those who were interested in the period and the selected texts seemed to have made more use of the Web resources, while a student who suggested that "maybe more background is needed" mentioned only the University Library when evaluating resources, even though explicitly invited to comment on the Web as well (where more background *was* provided). A student who described the website as "excellent and very helpful," on the other hand, was also able to volunteer informed opinion on the use of Electronic Key Texts. Another wondered if lecture notes could also be mounted on the website. Students who were enthusiastic about studying medieval texts enjoyed the range of resources available, while some of those who felt intimidated did not want to encounter even more information on a new and complex area.

Use of the website also seemed to map on to progress in students' ability to assess their own learning practices and apply specific learning processes to the modules they studied. At intermediate level, a strong bias towards the Library was evident in the resource evaluation, and students tended to focus on their own experiences of module content and not to mention the website at all. Their responses could be classed in simple terms as representing an "elaborative" learning style, marking them as "productive thinkers who individualise their understanding through personal language, and by relating the information they are learning to personal experience" (Ashman & Conway 1997: 134). By contrast, a large proportion of higher-level students did refer to the website; they were also more likely to discuss module structure and learning issues. These students displayed the characteristics of a "deep" learning style: they were able to "focus on concepts, organise ideas into networks, and analyse and synthesise material to ensure full understanding" (Ashman & Conway 1997: 134). Productive use of the website, then, was connected to the acquisition of higher-level learning skills in general; those students who got most from it used it to promote the construction of networks of ideas and analysis, rather than as a source of reproducible information. Thus the website responded to the learning of processing skills by encouraging students to make active choices about their interaction with the material.

Lessons learnt

In assessing the outcomes of the model as an e-Learning intervention, HEFCE's "Effective Practice with e-Learning—Effective Practice Evaluator" table was extremely useful. The structure of a website can help to organise and make coherent the structure of a module; it requires aims and objectives to be made unambiguous, but still allows for individual exploration and development of the subject. With core provision in particular, a range of student knowledge and interest levels must be catered for, and this includes a certain amount of student choice in the texts and subjects occupying most time and resources. In particular, some student choice as to medieval texts themselves seemed important: one student claimed to have "loved Chaucer" but found "all religious revelation Dull Dull Dull" [*sic*]. Another, however "felt a little 'Chaucered to death' halfway through" but still concluded "otherwise a fun module"! The range of Middle English texts now available on-line allows students to broaden their reading, whether or not "all the books have already been taken out of the Library" (a common student complaint), and to pursue related texts and information on the authors and subjects they enjoy most. In "Reinventing English", some students were drawn to the verse romances, while others greeted the appearance of Margery Kempe in "Authorising English" with shouts of joy, and yet others with sighs of exasperation. Many students were happy to opt for the bawdy, comic aspects of the *Canterbury Tales*, but found the religious aspects more of a challenge, perhaps because the amount of background knowledge involved in comprehending the Christian context can seem daunting at first. The diversity of interest in different aspects of Middle English literature would be difficult to support using traditional methods, but is more easily accommodated through the Web. The demands of the modern curriculum leave little time for the centuries of medieval literature we have to offer; the opportunity to design modules that build in access to e-texts and an element of student choice is one way of redressing the balance.

A corollary of this flexibility is that the use of electronic resources assumes a degree of learner independence. Effective exploitation of all the Web has to offer is related to students' awareness of their own best practice for learning. Further, those who know how to focus their ideas, what kinds of connections they are interested in and why, and how to collate and analyse material are well equipped to respond; those who see learning as merely a process of consumption and regurgitation will need to gain an understanding of these processes. Independent learning is something we encourage from the moment students first arrive, but it takes time for them to become reflective practitioners, and to develop a consciousness of their learning skills and preferences. Hence, some kind of mediation is required, especially for learners at earlier stages in the degree programme. The use of carefully-designed learning objects is one way of doing this; provision such as our "Key words and concepts" can provide a safe way of encountering and using different kinds of media and levels of "information" within a structured on-line environment.

At another level, this type of mediation can be integrated into the use of the blended model by giving tutors an opportunity to invite reflection and analysis of particular Web materials within the face-to-face context of the seminar room. Our intermediate-level students liked to collect specific, fact-based knowledge (Middle English language, author biographies) since it enabled them to feel that they were "doing something" in a new area and could measure their achievement. This enabled them to become competent in certain respects, but we also wanted them to develop their understanding rather than merely personalising it. However, this was a challenge to some: to approach and judge different kinds of Web material (scholarly articles and on-line journals, discussion lists and digitised images, for example) took them a long way out of their "safety zone" unless the analysis was initially carried through in seminars in traditional discussion. Yet it was a vital part of the learning process in a Web-based world and also constituted training for working with other e-resources; further, to "evaluate and critique" is included among Ohlsson's "epistemic tasks" for the production of discourse (Ohlsson 1995: 51). Further possibilities included setting tasks such as the evaluation of particular e-resources, as is often integrated into VLE courses, but bringing discussion of the outcomes into the seminar room rather than on-line (for a discussion of the relationships between teaching and learning, see Fowler & Mayes). This remains important; students spend ever more time on-line and increasing numbers of modules require them to interact with tutors and one another electronically. In addition to avoiding "email/discussion list fatigue," they also need to gain the confidence to talk directly about texts and the things they have learnt about them. Mixing on-line resources with face-to-face responses can offer much-needed variety to Web-weary students and provoke them to reassessment rather than simple acceptance of the content and presentation of information.

Conclusions

It is now five years since the initial design and implementation of these websites, a long time in relation to the ever-widening range of ICT. Even in this period, students have arrived showing more expertise in their use of on-line resources, and higher expectations as to what will be possible and/or available in their learning environments. As a result, we are now redesigning our Web provision to take account of the full integration of WebCT into the University's learning, teaching and administrative structures; this redesign has also to take account of curriculum change and the implications of ongoing research into improved techniques for on-line learning and the use of e-resources. The recent rebranding of the University is another consideration, as the pages have to be redesigned to the new standard. However, a recent assessment of the medieval Web provision has concluded that the structure of the sites is sound and that, with a little adjustment, they can continue to address the requirements both of students and of new medieval modules in our Department.

This period has also taught me a great deal about the use of electronic resources and their integration into my own teaching plans and techniques. The use of computer-mediated teaching and learning through VLEs appears to be spreading, and certainly my own experience with TopClass has convinced me of the potential effectiveness of this approach. However, designing and working with the websites has shown me that a variety of learning opportunities is increasingly important as VLEs become more widespread. Further, in some instances students prefer *not* to encounter material in this context, but to go directly to a website instead. As the majority of students now have access to and experience of the Web, they are familiar and comfortable with a series of interlinked pages and sites through which they can make their own way—not least without having to comment on everything they look at or prove that they have been there. This seems to me of prime importance when teaching Chaucer and other medieval literature to nonspecialist students who have not necessarily chosen to study these texts. In a familiar on-line environment, academically focused but not entirely divorced from students' informal surfing practice, the necessary range of pictorial, historical and textual resources can be accessed, and students can be reassured that there *is* enough material available to enable them to engage with the module and the period.

While focused, directed learning and teaching is our goal most of the time, there is also a great deal to be said for student choice and the ways in which it promotes independent learning, even with the constraints of a carefully-selected set of material ordered according to the needs of a module. Moreover, it is still the case that a broader background may also be acquired simply through non-specific browsing of a website, of the kind that many students still practise around the library shelves devoted to their subject area. If we are increasingly to encourage our students to take responsibility for and control of their own learning, we have to build models that enable them to do that to some extent, and do not necessarily police their every move in the process. For me, the experience of designing and watching students use these websites has reinforced the notion that one should not "take too narrow a view of what constitutes e-learning, or of where its main value might lie" (Mayes & de Freitas: 4). In the end, our students' learning should be as richly varied as the medieval literature we ask them to study.

Note

1. Since publishers are making a growing number of critical works available in electronic form through institutional subscriptions, recent secondary literature may also be accessed electronically; this cannot, of course, undo the importance of the library in preserving both earlier work and the history of scholarship in the discipline.

Works cited

Ashman, Adrian F. & Robert N. F. Conway (1997). *An Introduction to Cognitive Education*. London: Routledge

Brewer, Derek (2000). *The World of Chaucer*. Cambridge: D. S. Brewer

The Chaucer MetaPage (2006.6.1)
http://www.unc.edu/depts/chaucer/index.html

Fowler, Chris & Terry Mayes. "JISC e-Learning Models Desk Study: Stage 2: Mapping Theory to Practice and Practice to Tool Functionality Based on the Practitioner's Perspective," Joint Information Systems Committee, 8

Fox, Seamus & Kay MacKeogh (2003). "Can eLearning Promote Higher-order Learning Without Tutor Overload?", *Open Learning*, 18.2: 121–34

The Great Vowel Shift (2006.6.1)
http://facweb.furman.edu/~mmenzer/gvs/

The Harvard Chaucer site (2006.6.1)
http://www.courses.fas.harvard.edu/~ chaucer/

Harvard Chaucer pages on "Language and Linguistics" (2006.6.1)
http://www.courses. fas.harvard.edu/~chaucer/lang_ling.html

HEFCE *"Effective Practice with e-Learning—Effective Practice Evaluator" Table* (2005.19.12)
http://www.jisc.ac.uk/index.cfm?name=elp_practice

Koper, Rob (2001). *Modelling units of study from a pedagogical perspective: the pedagogical meta-model behind EML*
Retrieved on 2006.13.1 from:
http://www.learningnetworks.org/downloads/ped-metamodel.pdf

Littlejohn, Alison (2004). "The Effectiveness of Resources, Tools and Support Services used by Practitioners in Designing and Delivering e-Learning Activities: Final Report", *Joint Information Systems Committee*

The Luminarium site (2006.6.1)
http://www.luminarium.org/medlit/chaucer.htm

Manning, Richard D., Maxine S. Cohen, & Robert L. DeMichiell (2003). "Distance Learning: Step by Step", *Journal of Information Technology Education*, 2: 115–30: Retrieved on 2006.5.1 from:
http://jite.org/documents/Vol2/v2p115-130-96.pdf

Mayes, Terry & Sara de Freitas. "JISC e-Learning Models Desk Study: Stage 2: Review of e-Learning Theories, Frameworks and Models", *Joint Information Systems Committee*, 4: 1–32

Middle English Dictionary (2006.6.1)
http://ets.umdl.umich.edu/m/med

Ohlsson, S. (1995). "Learning to Do and Learning to Understand: A Lesson and Challenge for Cognitive Modelling", in *Learning in Humans and Machines: Towards an Interdisciplinary Learning Science*. London: Pergamon

O'Neill, Kayte, Gurmak Singh, & John O'Donoghue (2004). "Implementing E-learning Programmes for Higher Education: A Review of the Literature", *Journal of Information Technology Education*, 3: 313–23

Pearsall, Derek, ed. (1999). *Chaucer to Spenser: An Anthology of Writings in English 1375–1575*. Oxford: Blackwell

Reasons, Saxon G., Kevin Valadares, & Michael Slavkin (2005). "Questioning the Hybrid Model: Student Outcomes in Different Course Formats", *Journal of Asynchronous Learning Networks*: Retrieved on 2006.9.1 from: http://www.sloan-c.org/publications/jaln/v9n1/v9n1_reasons.asp#reasons5

Semper, Philippa (2005). "Electronic Resources", in *Chaucer*, ed. Ellis. Oxford: Oxford University Press: pp. 607–19; Retrieved on 2006.2.1 from: http:// www.oup.com/uk/booksites/content/0199259127/chapter36.pdf?version=1

9
Chaucer and the Visual Image: Learning, Teaching, Assessing

Lesley Coote

A comprehensive course which sought to fully understand the works of Geoffrey Chaucer should contain samples from all his works: *Troilus and Criseyde, Legend of Good Women, Romaunt of the Rose, Boece, Book of the Duchess* . . . Being an advocate for the absolute brilliance of this writer, why is there so much emphasis on the *Canterbury Tales* in my teaching?

The main reasons—or maybe excuses—lie in the diversity of the student body in classes at the University of Hull's Department of English, where any one seminar class of sixteen to twenty students contains a variety of abilities, ages, backgrounds and learning styles, so much so that the main problem is one of cognition; how to make them understand what makes me so passionate about this man and his work? I use the *Canterbury Tales* because they themselves are so diverse. On the most basic of levels, students are able more easily to identify, to feel comfortable with, a work which contains in its title the name of somewhere which still exists, of which they have heard if not seen, and the name of an individual "author." As a rule, twenty-first-century readers negotiate authenticity around the identity of a named individual author; of course, in Chaucer's own time writers (and indeed Chaucer himself) situated their claims to *auctoritas* in other areas, such as their place within a tradition of great writers, thinkers and scholars, but it can be difficult to enthuse modern students with the title of "anonymous." Most students confronted with Chaucer's work, however, will have some awareness of Chaucer's existence as a writer. This will be particularly true of the *Canterbury Tales*, at least one story from which will have been studied by many of them as part of their A-Level work.

In addition, the *Canterbury Tales* are in themselves so brilliantly diverse in their style, form, characterisations and settings that they provide an introduction and back-reference points for just about anything medieval. They have very strong narratives, which relate well to students' desires for "story" rather than "form" (which is easier to introduce if the narrative is strong, easy to follow and has clear pathways and resolutions). The tales are mostly relatively short (the *Knight's Tale* excepted, of course) and self-contained (yet framed and linked within another strong narrative line), making it easier to convince students that cognition and understanding are more comfortably possible for them; they seem to be "manageable."

All the ideas and methodologies contained in this article have been tested by action research over the years 2000–2004 in the Departments of English and Film Studies at the University of Hull, which has a commitment to widening participation and student diversity. The classes and seminar groups involved contain a majority of students between the ages of eighteen and twenty-two, with a majority being female. There are, however, increasingly large minorities of young male students, mature students of both sexes, and students with some form of learning challenge, the most common of which are dyslexia and dyspraxia. The curriculum is semesterised and modularised, and conforms to the British Level system: Level Four (first year undergraduate), Level Five (second year undergraduate), Level Six (third/fourth year undergraduate).

Visually-based presentations to virtual learning environment

At the same time as enabling students to learn and be excited about the *Canterbury Tales* and Chaucer in particular, and the medieval in general, the transferable skills agenda cannot be ignored (especially so in the light of Personal Development Planning requirements). Having already been using presentations in assessment, Internet communications for keeping in touch with students who mostly gathered together on campus only for two-hour classes, and the Web for research resources, it seemed a logical next step to begin harnessing communications and information technology for learning and teaching purposes. This led to greater and greater involvement with the visual image as a learning and teaching aid. The first step was to make the use of at least one electronic medium compulsory for student class presentations, which had to contain an element of the visual. This produced interesting, unlooked-for insights, such as the "performance" of the *Reeve's Tale* by a small army of fashion dolls on a table top, and an exposition of the *Nun's Priest's Tale* as peeling back the layers of an onion. These seem simple and silly, but the *Reeve's Tale* relies on careful spatial measurement and placing, along with perfect timing, and the *Nun's Priest's Tale* contains the elements of many different genres, all hidden inside one another, within the "skin" of a simple beast fable. We live, as Richard Howells (2003) has said, within a visual culture, possibly the most visual since the Middle Ages themselves, and images are much more familiar to some students than the book.

The next step was to transport these ideas, and to open up new possibilities, by the use of a virtual learning environment. This provided the ability to create direct links to important Chaucer websites and resources, communications facilities, and a discussion board. Each week's work could be situated in a weekly folder, for round-the-clock access. Feedback indicated that this was extremely popular with students, as student numbers doubled as the module became quickly filled to capacity, despite the need to read in Middle English. Interesting comments were made by mature students and those with learning challenges. The first group said that they had a greater sense of "belonging" to the group, as they could join the site from home when caring for small children, and receive my weekly "announcements." Dyslexic students said that the ability to access notes and other material as and when they needed it was particularly useful for them. It is always necessary, of course, to provide essential materials in hard copy for photocopying by those who need to, as not all students have equal access to computer hardware and/or software, or have broadband connections—a factor which is increasingly important when embedding film in virtual learning environments for student access.

Another important facility offered by the VLE was the ability to produce and import what I called "factfiles." These were small, gobbet-sized files of information, the purpose of which was to provide students with valuable background information for the study of the *Tales*, which otherwise would have to be gleaned from reading large amounts of text in books, much of which would be discarded (and hence the reading would not be undertaken in the first place). These factfiles included information conveyed by visual image and supporting text, or simply text with illustrative images. On the closed VLE, it was possible to use stills taken from the BBC's *Animated Canterbury Tales*, captured under the university's ERA licence. These were supported by images from a personal collection of photographs. Each factfile contained just enough information to be "digestible" and to convey valuable and useful information, but was not long enough to replace reading, always a danger with this type of resource. A bibliography offered suggestions for further reading to those interested enough in the topic. It was possible in this way to introduce cultural, social and historical information which might otherwise take valuable seminar time, become a distraction, or be ignored. In addition to these, factfiles were added on useful areas of literary theory, such as liminality theory, myth theory, feminist theory, monster theory, structuralist theory, and of course, Freud and Lacan. Another species of factfile included explanations of genres, and an opportunity to investigate different arrangements of the *Tales*, given the fact that only some of them can be ordered using Chaucer's own "clues." This can be done visually, using images of the pilgrims and descriptions—or visual representations— of their tale contents, arranged in their procession, with explanations for the ordering. This is a very good "rounding off" exercise for the last session, giving rise to plenty of debate. VLEs such as Blackboard also provide facilities for on-line quizzes, whether multiple choice, true/false or short essay. This did not seem very promising for literary studies, until it was tried as a means of "encouraging" students to read their texts, something which experience demonstrates has become more difficult over the past five years or so. A multiple choice/ true or false quiz based upon factual knowledge of the set texts, administered in the second or third week of a course, particularly if a small number of credits are awarded in respect of it, has turned out to be very popular (getting credits for factual knowledge) and useful (by the third or fourth week of term, the tutor is working with students who actually have some degree of knowledge of the texts).

Virtual learning environment to Web

Having built a Canterbury Tales VLE, the opportunity presented itself to adapt these features for a Web resource, which I then undertook in association with Brett Lucas, learning technology specialist at the English Subject Centre at Royal Holloway, University of London. There were time and budgetary constraints involved; a very small budget and a matter of months to do the work. The project thus became an exemplar for how any practitioner with a little knowledge of Web creation software and some raw materials might produce an Internet resource for themselves without external funding. This needed to contain all the elements of the VLE, whilst utilising any advantages conveyed by the alternative format. The resource was to be based upon Chaucer's *Canterbury Tales*, and was intended to enable students to read and enjoy the *Tales*, in order to aid overall understanding of the subject, whilst maybe encouraging them to read and to know more (and suggesting further avenues of inquiry). It would also need to respond to the needs of teachers for a flexible teaching resource. Besides this, teachers below Level Five and general readers/browsers might find it interesting and useful. Aimed also at the need for transferable skills, the site also needed some developmental material, so items on how to write essays and how to interpret and use images would be included. The main brief for the resource was that it should be visually rich, so the last feature, along with plenty of images to read, was necessary.

Images proved to be the major problem, as ERA material is copyright-protected on the Web (in fact, much material is copyright-protected on the Web). This was addressed by the use of private photographs taken by known individuals who had given their consent for their use. This did mean that more creativity was needed than if it had been possible to use manuscript illustrations, for example, but these would not have been within the budget of this project, or of the unfunded, or underfunded, practitioner. Although there are many images on the site, it is possible to use the text or ideas, whilst substituting other available images. The images were scanned or downloaded, then saved as full-sized TIFF images. This takes up a lot of space on the computer drive, but ensures full quality. They were then adapted, customised and compressed in an appropriate programme; the compression cutting down the amount of drive space very considerably. In some cases the brightness, colour balance and saturation was altered, and the contrast changed to give an impression (in the case of a painting for example) of original colour, although sacrificing accuracy somewhat in the cause of interest. For purposes of Internet use, compressed images, such as JPEG, are good enough for such use, as they are for use on a VLE; it is when they are to be used in printed form that a better image may be helpful.

With a VLE, the mode of presentation is often prescribed, or at least restricted, by the formats which have been programmed into it, leaving little to the imagination apart from what to use as the banner on the introductory page, what to insert into files and where. Navigation is similarly prescribed. One of the attractions of a website is that this is not the case; the pages are a blank slate onto which anything may be inscribed according to the purpose of the site, and the creativity of the programmer—within the parameters of his/her ability to manipulate available software. Alongside scholarly aims, many of the principles of commercial design also apply. For the "average" user, a site has to be attractive and engaging, easy to use, without being overloaded with textual information or complex graphics. It should stimulate "gist" learning, that is, selection of knowledge in order to create an overall picture of the topic in question, rather than to simply be a quarry for specific items of knowledge, in which case it would cease to be a learning resource and become a research tool.

Items such as factfiles (on medieval pilgrimage, the Hundred Years' War, the Black Death, the Arthurian legend, alchemy, medieval towns and cities, religious orders, and so on) can be transported from a VLE, and back again, but the length needs to be carefully adjusted, and some images could be added to make the files more attractive and engaging for readers, as well as to be illustrative or explanatory. In this case, a longer file, with illustrations, on the life of Chaucer was also included. A site needs to have an overall arrangement, and this was done by grouping and adapting the factfiles and the individual characters and tales into a series of "worlds" based upon Estates Satire, after the groupings suggested by Jill Mann (1973), but not slavishly replicating them. An explanation was provided, with an invitation to consider other ways of grouping the stories, as the method chosen was not chosen for its imaginative approach, but its practicality and the nature of the available images. Under this heading the *Tales* were listed, each linked to discussion points, genre information and basic literary theories, as on the VLE, as tools to enable independent interpretation. There was only time to include a general bibliography, but this is desirable too, linked to each tale (even if the items are repeated). This, then, provides a "package" for the student, and for the tutor, from the schoolteacher to the inexperienced graduate tutor and the harassed lecturer, when pressed for time and looking for immediately usable material, and/or an immediately usable framework on which to "hang" the material, or the knowledge and expertise, they already have.

The immediate, and obvious, advantage of web pages over virtual learning environments is the flexibility of their navigation. Navigation is all-important in a website, and this was planned first, as soon as the basic page ideas were in place. Some virtual learning environments, such as Merlin, enable the instructor to build in student pathways, but the benefit of the website is that it can provide a number of possible pathways, alongside entirely free choice, and the pathways may be dispensed with whenever the user wishes. In accordance with this, and the objectives of the site, pathways were created to provide a guided introduction for new users, but free movement around the site for the more experienced. The pathways were provided with introductions, one for the student user and one for the practitioner user, and an overall instruction page was provided for all users, essential to explain what the site is about, for whom it is intended and how to use it. This enables all users to go immediately to what they want or need, and those looking for something else—for example, a "research-based" site such as Harvard or the Metapage, to go elsewhere. Links to these sites were, however, provided from this site, for those who then wish to pass on to more challenging material. Navigation needs to be obvious, attractive and simple at the same time, without overcrowding the page. Navigation buttons within the *Tales* section were provided at the top and base of each page (always in the same position and using the same image for the same link), created by taking slices from digitised photographic material. Links to other sections of the site were placed, conventionally, at the top of the page. Pathways were indicated by an "on to next page" arrow at the base of each page, but the navigation buttons and links at the base and top of the page would enable the user to leave the pathway at any time, thus building up a "gist" picture of the topic overall. A forum for comments should be provided; within a university learning situation, they can take the place of discussion boards, are much easier to use, and can be arranged like MUDS (multi-user dungeons) for anonymous, "fun" conversation in a prearranged setting such as a bar or a lounge, a castle or the Tabard Inn . . . Forum software is available cheaply or as free downloads from the Internet. A small, but important caveat when using this is to check that the format is supported by the server you intend to use; institutional servers such as those provided by universities, although they will support most, do not always support *all* forum software.

On the basis that it is important for students to feel that they can read and understand Chaucerian Middle English, the *General Prologue* was introduced in both text and sound. This was done by the inclusion of a Flash facility, downloadable by users, which enabled them to listen to a reading of the Prologue, whilst having the choice of actually reading the text in either modern English or Middle English, at the same time. In this way, the new reader can look at and listen to the modern version first, whilst gradually switching the visual to Chaucer's own language, all the time retaining the ability to switch back and check the modern translation. We were lucky enough to obtain the services of a professional actor, John Wesley Harris, to read the Prologue for us; unfortunately, time constraints meant that we could not do the same for all the *Tales*. Due to improvements in virtual learning environment programmes, this can now be accomplished either on a webpage or by using text and WAV files inserted into a VLE folder. The reading can be provided by the tutor or others, in both modern and medieval English, whilst the student reads a choice of text, or views images—or both. The readings can also be downloaded onto DVD, CD or iPod, for students without computer access. At around this time, I was also offered the opportunity to produce a low-priced edition of the *Canterbury Tales*, suitable for students and the general reader. The base text was British Library MS Harley 7334, which I transcribed and modified from Hengwrt. I included the "discussion points" and an introduction for each *Tale*; however, although it was necessary to modernise the punctuation, nothing was translated. The idea was to make the reading easier for those unused to medieval English by placing the difficult words in bold type, with a translation in the margin on the same line. In this way, the reader's eye, moving (in Western culture) from left to right, catches sight of the translation in the same movement as the word itself, thus creating an impression of having "read" it. It might be objected that this privileges certain words and phrases, but it has been proved from feedback that this does work. Notes and glosses on the same page, to avoid unnecessary turning to the back of the book, also help greatly. Gradually, the more common words can be dropped from the marginalia, as the reader gains in competence. It is possible to do this with shorter texts on a webpage or in a VLE, although the printed page is still the most ergonomically friendly way to disseminate the larger text. It is possible to produce printed material in this way, linked to pages on a website or VLE, though (again, I have done this with Chaucerian, and other, material).

Electronic tools to film and new media

From this position, I have more recently progressed to the importation of techniques and methodologies from film studies and creative writing, both to enhance the learning experience in literary studies, and also to vary the types of assessment available. The object of this is to benefit students for whom essay writing may not show their abilities to best effect, and to challenge students used to writing essays to extend their abilities, make new discoveries, and obtain some very useful transferable skills. The idea of providing "alternatives" to the essay, with carefully-considered assessment criteria, is one that I am currently investigating.

Using still images captured from film and digitised

Film stills, alone or in groups, make very good starting-points for discussion. They can also be grouped in interesting ways. For example, an image taken from the BBC's *Animated Canterbury Tales* of the *Knight's Tale* of Arcite brandishing his sword in the contest with Palamon, gives rise to very different insights when paired or grouped with Arcite and

Palamon as friends, Arcite or Arcite and Palamon with Duke Theseus, Saturn with his "grandchildren," and/or Arcite feminised and dressed androgynously as Emelye's squire (beautifully portrayed with "girly" puffed sleeves in the BBC version). These images all occur in the one Tale, but themes can be addressed by pairing the same image with the Miller's Absolon with his ploughshare, the decrepit January in the *Merchant's Tale*, or Chaucer's own Knight and Squire. These may be used as class resources, but can also form the basis for essays or paragraph studies, as assessment.

Exercises in adaptation are fraught with pitfalls, as different media such as film and written text require different interpretative tools (and it is necessary always to be aware of this). However, it is possible, for example, to select and display stills which demonstrate the film-maker's choices and interpretations. The use of the flower, which falls and withers when the young woman is raped by the knight, then springs into bloom again when he marries the hag in the BBC animated *Wife of Bath's Tale*, is a good example of this. Does the flower represent virginity, or maybe the spirit of the young woman, or maybe it represents Woman or the spirit of Woman, or maybe simply goodness or some other abstract quality? Is it right to show it returning to life and vigour at the end, and is such a resolution possible anyway? Does such a resolution exist in Chaucer's story or his intent?

Remaining with the Wife of Bath, stills can also be "glosed" by placing them on a table or page, or in the centre of an interactive whiteboard, then inviting the group to place their own comments and ideas as marginalia around them. This is also a good visual aid for essay writing, but can also be used as part of an assessed exercise, which may be written as an essay, or in some other form such as paragraphs or bulleted notes, or paragraphs of text displayed with the image.

Analysis of digitised film clips

This is another useful technique imported from film studies. It involves the extraction and analysis of a short piece of film, usually about one to three minutes long, often a short scene. This can then be analysed according to criteria such as those given in Appendix B. For students with no film studies background it is necessary to avoid more technical areas of analysis, replacing them with literary connections. This type of work may be used to introduce students, who live a modern visual culture, to the "ways of seeing" with which medieval people viewed images. Using a VLE, a short clip can now be inserted into a file as an MPEG document, so it is possible to produce and circulate exempla in this way. Such an example would consist of a short embedded clip, followed by suggestions for analysis, accompanied by still images taken from the same clip. Again, something similar can be produced as assessed work.

Writing and producing digitised material

A recent venture for Level Six students at Hull is the use of student-authored digital material as part of their assessment. This takes place in a module where selected stories from Chaucer are used with other medieval material and medievalist films (including the *Animated Pardoner's Tale*) to explore a theme, in this case the idea of "death and the devil" in medieval text and medievalist film. The assessment is divided into two parts, in order not to disadvantage those who perform best when writing essays. Half the module mark, therefore, is based upon an essay, which may or may not be based upon film stills, but the other half consists of a project, ideally carried out in twos or threes, in which the group has to address one of a set of given options, which are:

- Create an idea for (not write the whole of . . .) a screenplay or story-board for an adaptation of one of the module's set texts, e.g. the *Dance of Death*, Raoul de Houdenc's *Songe d'Enfer* (*Vision of Hell*), Chaucer's *Pardoner's Tale*, *Friar's Tale* or *Summoner's Tale*.
- Create a webpage or series of webpages, or Powerpoint slides, to address one of a set of questions based upon the module, relating to the topic.
- Create a plan for an exhibition or other display, addressing one of a set of questions based upon the module.

The group should make a short film of three to five minutes, which must form part of the project, or illustrate the storyboard, or be a "making of" documentary. Each project must be based upon the visual, but must also be accompanied by explanatory text, setting out the rationale for choices made and methodologies chosen. The whole must demonstrate a clear understanding of the topic or text, and the ability to express and explain within the medium or media selected; in effect, it must satisfy the same criteria as an essay, including research, without actually *being* an essay. Students are given basic instructions on how to use a camcorder (which some of them know anyway), download their material, and edit it using editing software. It is hoped that these skills will soon be embedded in the programme from Level Four. So far, this has proved extremely popular with students, and has produced some very good work, including work from students who do not perform to their best advantage in essay writing, but who have demonstrated a very good, clear understanding of the subject when given the opportunity to express themselves in an alternative way. Work is currently being undertaken on devising rigorous academic criteria for such assessments, which lately have included adaptations of the *Pardoner's Tale* set among local "bikers" in East Yorkshire, and among hippies at the Glastonbury Festival, as well as the *Songe d'Enfer* in prohibition Chicago or a "medieval" theme park!

Appendix A

Using VLE and other forms of IT:

- Some basic questions need to be asked. Can IT or use of a VLE help students to achieve the learning outcomes of the course or module? Do these include transferable skills, and if so, what are they to be? An external examiner needs to be able to moderate these.
- Balanced alongside more traditional methods, it has to be worth the time and trouble to learn to operate, then to introduce and (if necessary) train and equip students to use, and develop non-traditional, or electronic ones. It takes personal investment in time, commitment and reflective development to make this work.
- Students will need a guide on how to access the site or VLE. This will need to be printed for inclusivity. In a diverse student environment, not all may be confident with on-line information.
- A second guide, on-line, will be needed, telling students how their learning patterns may have to change and why, explaining the medium which they are using (for example, a guide to what a VLE is and how to use it for best effect). In addition, it may be helpful to add explanations of "gist" learning and how the Internet can help the individual student to understand in this way. A guide to "how to get the best out of the Internet" can also be useful, such as how to evaluate websites for learning, and what is meant by suffixes such as .gov, .org, and .edu. If students are not "gist" learners, they will be best helped by using the Internet for resource and communication, whilst following their own preferred methods of working. Many students are helped by Internet learning tools, but some are not. If the course, or part of the course, is to be examined by some visually based method, it may be necessary to include some form of written material which they, too, feel comfortable with, to prevent discrimination against those who may be very good students.

- Backup is always necessary. Widening participation leads to students who have less access to computing facilities at home. Networks crash, usually at the worst of times. Video CDs, DVDs, tapes and even hand-outs and OHPs can be a godsend at such times.
- VLEs may not be as good for communication as they seem. They work if students are used to using them, are only taking a few courses, or are distance learners. It helps if students are compelled to put their personal e-mail address into their "bank" of addresses; frequently they do not access departmental e-mail addresses. They will not always access the website for news, or look at what is not immediately visible on the first page. It may be necessary to use more conventional means of posting important notices, too. A good idea is to begin with an exercise (or two) which force the students to use the site, such as my on-line (factual) multiple choice quiz.
- Putting on lots of interesting information and web links is a good way to ensure that students access your site. Information sections (such as my factfiles) should not be too short not to be valuable as resources, but should not be so long that they discourage reading, and they should be visually attractive enough to encourage students to read them.
- VLEs and the Web really come into their own with visual analysis. In the latest versions of the Blackboard VLE video and audio files such as MPEG, AVI and WAV may be simply inserted. Any combination of these may be used, and students' own files may be added, either for general access or to group pages. Tapes, CDs or DVDs may be needed for home analysis, as some students may have access difficulties.
- Alternative text may be added to a VLE or website, but it should be short and visually attractive; an introduction should inform students how to use it.
- It is a good idea to add an announcement every time material is added to the site.
- An announcement should be added at least once a week during term, so that students know the tutors are interested in the site, and in their progress.
- If students are encouraged or compelled to make webpages or power-point displays for assessment purposes, the external examiner should express willingness to access and to moderate them in advance, to avoid difficulties later.
- Students may not progress very far, very fast. There are still a reasonable minority of students who are not comfortable with information technology.

- Students should be given time to learn and to develop expertise in using VLEs and web-based learning tools. The tutor/s should also be as well informed as possible about how things work, and not be totally reliant on technicians and other experts. It is only if you understand how a medium works (to a certain extent—not necessarily in an expert way) that you can work out how to use it to very best advantage in subject teaching. There is always room for further development.

Appendix B

Some ideas for clip analysis:

- Where does the scene occur in the film/text?
- Are any of the major themes of the film illustrated in this scene, and how is this done (refer to characters, dialogue, action, setting, *mise-en-scène*—or how objects and characters are placed and moved in the setting—symbolism, use of the set, camerawork and angles, colour, sound . . .). How does this interpret the text?
- What developments take place in the scene, and how do they "fit" into the rest of the film?
- How are characters illustrated in the scene, and how does this relate to the rest of the film?
- Can you make any interesting statements about the director's art—camerawork, set, *mise-en-scène*, editing or lack of it, etc., or any "tricks" which simply give pleasure to director and audience, and can you relate them to Chaucer's own art as demonstrated in the text?
- Does this scene, or the developments within it, have any symbolic or metaphorical (that is, deeper) meaning? How is this conveyed, and what might it be, and does the text/s have such meaning, also?
- Is there any theory you know which might be helpful in discussing this scene/text?
- Can you make any constructive comments about costume, makeup, props, lighting, music and sound, and can you relate this to the way in which Chaucer uses these elements in his text/s?

Works cited

The Chaucer MetaPage (2005.12.12)
   http://www.unc.edu/depts/chaucer/index.html
Harvard Chaucer pages on "Language and Linguistics" (2005.12.12)
   http://www.courses.fas.harvard.edu/~chaucer/lang_ling.html

Howells, Richard (2003). *Visual Culture*. Cambridge: Polity *Key Skills with Chaucer* (2005.12.12)
  http://www.english.heacademy.ac.uk/explore/resources/ index.php
Mann, Jill (1973). *Chaucer and Medieval Estates Satire: The Literature of Social Classes and the General Prologue to the Canterbury Tales*. Cambridge: Cambridge University Press

Bibliography

Ackroyd, Peter (2003). *The Clerkenwell Tales*. London: Chatto & Windus
Alpay, Esat (2005). "Group Dynamic Processes in Email Groups", *Active Learning in Higher Education*, 6.1: 7–16
Ashman, Adrian F. & Robert N. F. Conway (1997). *An Introduction to Cognitive Education*. London: Routledge
Auten, Janet Gebhart (2003). "Helping Students Decode the Difficult Text: 'The Yellow Wall-Paper' and the Sequential Response", in *The Pedagogical Wallpaper: Teaching Charlotte Perkins Gilman's "The Yellow Wall-Paper"*, ed. Jeffrey Andrew Weinstock. New York: Peter Lang: pp. 130–43
Badham, John, dir. (1977). *Saturday Night Fever*. Paramount Pictures
Bakhtin, Mikhail (1981). *The Dialogic Imagination: Four Essays*, ed. Michael Holquist, trans. Caryl Emerson & Michael Holquist. Austin: University of Texas Press
Bard, Imre (1986). "Sequencing the Writing of Essays in Pre-Modern World History Courses", *History Teacher*, 19: 361–71
Barr, Robert B. & John Tagg (1995). "From Teaching to Learning – A New Paradigm for Undergraduate Education", *Change*, 27.6: 13–25
Baugh, A. C., ed. (1963). *Chaucer's Major Poetry*. Englewood Cliffs, NJ: Prentice-Hall
Baxter Magolda, Marcia B. (2002). *Making Their Own Way: Narratives for Transforming Higher Education to Promote Self-development*. Sterling, VA: Stylus
———. & Jennifer Buckley (March 1997). "Constructive-developmental Pedagogy: Linking Knowledge Construction and Students' Epistemological Development", Paper Presented at the Annual Meeting of the American Educational Research Association, Chicago, IL
Beidler, Peter (1996). "Teaching Chaucer as Drama: The Garden Scene in 'The Shipman's Tale' ", *Exemplaria* (Teaching Chaucer in the 90s), 8.2: 485–93
Benson, C. David (1986). *Chaucer's Drama of Style: Poetic Variety and Contrast in the "Canterbury Tales"*. Chapel Hill: University of North Carolina Press
Benson, Larry D. *Glossarial DataBase of Middle English*
www.hti.umich.edu/g/gloss/
———. ed. (1987). *The Riverside Chaucer*. Oxford: Oxford University Press
Bergson, Henri (1912). *Laughter: An Essay on the Meaning of the Comic*, trans. Cloudesley Brereston & Fred Rothwell. New York: Macmillan
Blakemore Evans, G., ed. (1974). *The Riverside Shakespeare*, The Riverside Shakespeare. Boston: Houghton Mifflin
Bloch, Howard (Fall 1989). "Chaucer's Maiden's Head: *The Physician's Tale* and the Poetics of Virginity", *Representations*, 28: 113–34
Boccaccio, Giovanni (1972). *The Decameron*, trans. G. H. McWilliam. Harmondsworth: Penguin
———. (1986). *Il Filostrato*, Italian text ed. Vincenzo Pernicone, trans. Robert P. ApRoberts & Anna Bruni Seldis. New York: Garland Publishing Inc.
Boccaccio, Giovanni (2001). *Famous Women [De claris mulieribus]*, ed. and trans. Virginia Brown. Cambridge, MA and London: Harvard University Press

Boitani, Piero & Jill Mann, eds (2003). *The Cambridge Companion to Chaucer*, 2nd edn. Cambridge: Cambridge University Press

Brewer, Derek (2000). *The World of Chaucer*. Cambridge: D. S. Brewer

Broad, Martin, Marian Matthews, & Andrew McDonald (2004). "Active Learning in Higher Education", *Accounting Education Through an Online-Supported Virtual Learning Environment*, 5.2: 135–51

Brown, Peter, ed. (2002). *A Companion to Chaucer*. Oxford: Blackwell

Brown, Scott C. (2004). "Learning Across the Campus: How College Facilitates the Development of Wisdom", *Journal of College Student Development*, 45: 134–48

Bryan, W. F. & Germaine Dempster, eds (1941). *Chaucer: Sources and Analogues*, rpt New York: Humanities Press, 1958

Burger, Glenn (2003). *Chaucer's Queer Nation*. Minneapolis and London: University of Minnesota Press

——— & Steven F. Kruger (2003). "Queer Chaucer in the Classroom", in *Teaching Literature: A Companion*, ed. Tanya Agothocleous & Ann C. Dean. Basingstoke: Palgrave Macmillan: pp. 31–40

Burnley, J. D. (1982). "Inflexion in Chaucer's Adjectives", *Neuphilologische Mitteilungen*, 83: 169–77

———. (1983). *A Guide to Chaucer's Language*. Basingstoke: Macmillan—now Palgrave Macmillan

Camargo, Martin (2005). "The State of Medieval Studies: A Tale of Two Universities", *Studies in the Age of Chaucer*, 27: 239–47

Cannon, Christopher (1998). *The Making of Chaucer's English: A Study of Words*. Cambridge: Cambridge University Press

———. (2003). "Chaucer's Style", in *Cambridge Companion to Chaucer*, ed. Boitani & Mann: pp. 233–50

Carruthers, Mary (1979). "The Wife of Bath and the Painting of Lions", *Publications of the Modern Language Association of America*, 94: 209–22

———. (1990). *The Book of Memory: A Study of Memory in Medieval Culture*. Cambridge: Cambridge University Press

Coghill, Nevill (1960). *The Canterbury Tales Translated into Modern English*. London: Penguin

Coles Jr, W. E. (1970). "The Sense of Nonsense as a Design for Sequential Writing Assignments", *College Composition and Communication*, 21: 27–34

Cowen, Janet & George Kane, eds (1995). *The Legend of Good Women*. East Lansing, MI: Colleagues Press

Crane, Susan (2002). *The Performance of Self: Ritual, Clothing, and Identity During the Hundred Years War*. Philadelphia: University of Pennsylvania Press

Curran, Terrie (1980). "The Cultural Context", in *Approaches*, ed. Gibaldi. New York: The Modern Language Association of America: pp. 97–104

Dinshaw, Carolyn (1989). *Chaucer's Sexual Poetics*. Madison: University of Wisconsin Press

Donaldson, E. Talbot (1985). *The Swan at the Well: Shakespeare Reading Chaucer*. New Haven: Yale University Press

Elbow, Peter (2002). "High Stakes and Low Stakes in Assigning and Responding to Writing", in *Dialogue on Writing: Rethinking ESL, Basic Writing, and First-Year Composition*, ed. Geraldine DeLuca, Len Fox, Mark-Ameen Johnson, & Myra Kogen. Mahwah, NJ: Erlbaum: pp. 289–98

Ellis, Roger (2002). "Translation", in *Companion*, ed. Brown. Oxford: Blackwell: pp. 443–58

Ellis, Steve, ed. (1998). *Chaucer: The Canterbury Tales*. London and New York: Longman

———. (2000). *Chaucer at Large: The Poet in the Popular Imagination*. Minneapolis: University of Minnesota Press

———. ed. (2005). *Chaucer*. Oxford: Oxford University Press

Farrell, Thomas (1989). "Privacy and the Boundaries of Fabliau in the 'Miller's Tale' ", *English Literary History*, 56.4: 773–95

Field, Rosalind (2005). *Chaucer Teaching in UK Universities* http://www. oup.com/uk/booksites/content/0199259127/resources/ukuniversities.pdf

Findlay, L. M. (1999). "Reading and Teaching Troilus Otherwise: St Maure, Chaucer, and Henryson", *Florilegium*, 16: 61–75

Fletcher, Angus (1964). *Allegory: The Theory of a Symbolic Mode*. Ithaca: Cornell University Press

Folks, Cathalin B. (1996). "Of Sundry Folk: The Canterbury Pilgrimage as Metaphor for Teaching Chaucer at the Community College", *Exemplaria* (Teaching Chaucer in the 90s), 8.2: 473–7

Folsom, Marcia McClintock (2004). " 'I Wish We Had a Donkey': Small-Group Work and Writing Assignments for *Emma*", in *Approaches to Teaching Austen's Emma*, ed. Marcia McClintock Folsom. New York: Modern Language Association: pp. 159–68

Fowler, Chris & Terry Mayes. *JISC e-Learning Models Desk Study: Stage 2: Mapping Theory to Practice and Practice to Tool Functionality Based on the Practitioner's Perspective*, Joint Information Systems Committee, 8 vols

Fox, Seamus & Kay MacKeogh (2003). "Can eLearning Promote Higher-order Learning Without Tutor Overload?", *Open Learning*, 18.2: 121–34

Fradenburg, Louise O. (1989). "Criticism, Anti-Semitism and the *Prioress's Tale*", *Exemplaria*, 1: 69–115

Fradenburg, L. O. Aranye (2002). *Sacrifice Your Love: Psychoanalysis, Historicism, Chaucer*. Minneapolis and London: University of Minnesota Press

Freud, Sigmund (1960). *Jokes and their Relation to the Unconscious*, Standard Edition, vol. 8 (1905), trans. James Strachey. London: Hogarth Press

Frye, Northrop (1957). *Anatomy of Criticism: Four Essays*. Princeton: Princeton University Press

Furnivall, F. J., ed. (1868–84). *The Six-Text Edition of Chaucer's Canterbury Tales*, Chaucer Society 1st series. London: Trübner

Gadamer, Hans-Georg (1976). *Philosophical Hermeneutics*, trans. and ed. David E. Linge. Berkeley: University of California Press

———. (2003). *Truth and Method*, 2nd revsd edn, trans. Joel Weinsheimer & Donald Marshall. New York and London: Continuum Books

Gaipa, Mark (2004). "Breaking into the Conversation: How Students Can Acquire Authority for their Writing", *Pedagogy*, 4.3: 419–37

Gallop, Jane, ed. (1995). *Pedagogy: The Question of Impersonation*. Bloomington: Indiana University Press

Gardner, Howard (1995). "The Theory of Multiple Intelligences", in *Multiple Intelligences: A Collection*, ed. Robin Fogarty & James Bellanca. Arlington Heights, IL: IRI/Skylight Training and Publishing, Inc.

Gibaldi, Joseph, ed. (1980). *Approaches to Teaching Chaucer's Canterbury Tales*. New York: The Modern Language Association of America

Gibbs, Graham & Martin Coffey (2004). "The Impact of Training of University Teachers on their Teaching Skills, their Approaches to Teaching and the Approach to Learning of their Students", *Active Learning in Higher Education*, 5.1: 87–101

Gibson, Jonathan (2005). "Pedagogic Research in English", *English Subject Centre Newsletter*

Gilliam, Terry & Terry Jones, dirs (1975). *Monty Python and the Holy Grail*. Python (Monty) Pictures

Gokhale, Anuradha A. (1995). *Collaborative Learning Enhances Critical Thinking* http://scholar.lib.vt.edu/ejournals/JTE/jte-v7n1/gokhale.jte-v7n1.html

Goodman, Paul S. (1986). *Designing Effective Work Groups*, 1st edn. San Franciso: Jossey-Bass

Goodman, Thomas (1996). "On Literacy", *Exemplaria* (Teaching Chaucer in the 90s), 8.2: 459–72

Greenberg, Karen L. (1998). "Review: Grading, Evaluating, Assessing: Power and Politics in College Composition", *College Composition and Communication*, 49: 275–84

Greenblatt, Stephen (1988). *Shakespearean Negotiations*. Berkeley and Los Angeles: University of California Press

———. (1995). "Culture", in *Terms for Literary Study*, ed. Frank Lentricchia & Thomas McLaughlin. Chicago: Chicago University Press

Guskin, Alan (1994). "Reducing Student Costs and Enhancing Student Learning: The University Challenge of the 1990s. Part II: Restructuring the Role of Faculty", *Change*, 26.5: 16–25

Hagen, Susan K. (1996). "Interdisciplinary Chaucer", *Exemplaria* (Teaching Chaucer in the 90s), 8.2: 449–53

Hahn, Thomas (1992). "Teaching the Resistant Woman: The Wife of Bath and the Academy", *Exemplaria*, 4: 431–40

Hallissy, Margaret (1995). *A Companion to Chaucer's Canterbury Tales*. Westport, CT and London: Greenwood Press

Hansen, Elaine T. (2005). "Response: Chaucerian Values", *Studies in the Age of Chaucer*, 27: 277–87

Harty, Kevin J. (2005). "Chaucer in Performance", in *Chaucer*, ed. Ellis. Oxford: Oxford University Press: pp. 560–75

Heaney, Seamus (1999). *Beowulf*. London: Faber

Helgeland, Brian, dir. (2001). *A Knight's Tale*. Columbia Pictures

Horobin, Simon (2001). "J. R. R. Tolkien as a Philologist: A Reconsideration of the Northernisms in Chaucer's *Reeve's Tale*", *English Studies*, 82: 97–105

———. (2003). *The Language of the Chaucer Tradition*. Cambridge: D.S. Brewer

——— & Jeremy Smith (2002). *An Introduction to Middle English*. Edinburgh: Edinburgh University Press

Howells, Richard (2003). *Visual Culture*. Cambridge: Polity

Jauss, Hans Robert (1989). *Question and Answer: Forms of Dialogic Understanding*, trans. and ed. Michael Hays. Minneapolis: University of Minnesota Press

Johnson, D. W. & F. P. Johnson (2000). *Joining Together: Group Theory and Group Skills*. Boston, MA: Allyn and Bacon

Jones, Rowena Revis (1989). "Group Work as an Approach to Teaching Dickinson", in *Approaches to Teaching Dickinson's Poetry*, ed. Robin Riley Fast & Christine Mack Gordon. New York: Modern Language Association: pp. 62–9

Jost, Jean E. (2000). "Teaching *The Canterbury Tales*: The Process and The Product", *Studies in Medieval and Renaissance Teaching*, 8: 61–9

Kant, Emmanuel (1952). *Critique of Judgement*, trans. James Creed Meredith. Oxford: Clarendon Press

Katz, Joseph & Mildred Henry (1993). *Turning Professors into Teachers: A New Approach to Faculty Development and Student Learning*. Phoenix, AZ: American Council on Education and Oryx Press

Keating, Barbara (1991). "Using Staged Assignments as Student Spotters: Learning Research Methods", *Teaching Sociology*, 19: 514–17

Kegan, Robert (1994). *In Over Our Heads: The Mental Demands of Modern Life*. Cambridge, MA: Harvard University Press

Kinney, Clare R. (1996). "Theory and Pedagogy", *Exemplaria* (Teaching Chaucer in the 90s), 8.2: 455–7

Kirkpatrick, Graeme (2005). "Online 'Chat' Facilities as Pedagogic Tools: A Case Study", *Active Learning in Higher Education*, 6.2: 145–59

Knapp, Peggy A. (Fall 2000). "The Work of Alchemy", *Journal of Medieval and Early Modern Studies*, 30: 575–99

Knights, Ben (2005). "Foreword", *English Subject Centre Newsletter*, 9: 2–3

Koper, Rob (2001). *Modelling units of study from a pedagogical perspective: the pedagogical meta-model behind EML*:
http://www.learningnetworks.org/downloads/ped-metamodel.pdf

Laurillard, Diana (2002). *Rethinking University Teaching and Learning: A Conversational Framework for the Effective Use of Learning Technologies*. London: RoutledgeFalmer

Leicester Jr, H. Marshall (1980). "The Art of Impersonation: A General Prologue to *The Canterbury Tales*", *Publications of the Modern Language Association of America*, 95: 213–24

——. (1998). "Structure as Deconstruction", in *Chaucer: The Canterbury Tales*, ed. Ellis. London and New York: Longman: pp. 23–41

Littlejohn, Alison (2004). "The Effectiveness of Resources, Tools and Support Services used by Practitioners in Designing and Delivering e-Learning Activities: Final Report", *Joint Information Systems Committee*

Lockwood, Anne Turnbaugh (1993). "Multiple Intelligences in Action ('The MI Provocation' and 'The MI Key')", *Journal of Research and the Classroom*, 4: 1–12

Malone, Nolan, Kaari F. Baluja, Joseph M. Costanzo, & Cynthia J. Davis (December 2003). "The Foreign Born Population: 2000", *U.S. Census Bureau*:
http://www.census.gov/prod/2003pubs/c2kbr-34.pdf

Mann, Jill (1973). *Chaucer and Medieval Estates Satire: The Literature of Social Classes and the General Prologue to the Canterbury Tales*. Cambridge: Cambridge University Press

Manning, Richard D., Maxine S. Cohen, & Robert L. DeMichiell (2003). "Distance Learning: Step by Step", *Journal of Information Technology Education*, 2: 115–30

Mayes, Terry & Sara de Freitas. "JISC e-Learning Models Desk Study: Stage 2: Review of e-Learning Theories, Frameworks and Models", *Joint Information Systems Committee*, 4: 1–32

McInerney, Maud Burnett (2005). "Introduction", *Arthuriana*, 15: 1–5

Middle English Dictionary. Ann Arbor: University of Michigan Press, 1952–2001

Miller, Mark (2000). "Naturalism and its Discontents", *English Literary History*, 67: 1–44

Minkova, Donka (2005). "Chaucer's Language: Pronunciation, Morphology, Metre", in *Chaucer*, ed. Ellis: pp. 130–57

Muckle, J. T., trans. (1964). *The Story of Abelard's Adversities*. Toronto: Pontifical Institute of Medieval Studies

Ohlsson, S. (1995). "Learning to Do and Learning to Understand: A Lesson and Challenge for Cognitive Modelling", in *Learning in Humans and Machines: Towards an Interdisciplinary Learning Science*. London: Pergamon

Oizumi, Akio (1991). *A Complete Concordance to the Works of Geoffrey Chaucer*. Amsterdam: Hildesheim

O'Neill, Kayte, Gurmak Singh, & John O'Donoghue (2004). "Implementing E-learning Programmes for Higher Education: A Review of the Literature", *Journal of Information Technology Education*, 3: 313–23

Otte, George (1995). "In-voicing: Beyond the Voice Debate", in *Pedagogy*, ed. Gallop. Bloomington: Indiana University Press: pp. 147–54

Owst, G. R. (1933). *Literature and the Pulpit in Medieval England*. Cambridge: Cambridge University Press

Oxford English Dictionary, 2nd edition. Oxford: Oxford University Press, 1989

Panitz, Ted (1996). *A Definition of Collaborative vs Cooperative Learning* http://www.city.londonmet.ac.uk/deliberations/collaborativelearning/panitz2.html

Patterson, Lee (1996). "The Disenchanted Classroom", *Exemplaria* (Teaching Chaucer in the 90s), 8.2: 513–45

———. (1998). "The Subject of Confession: The Pardoner and the Rhetoric of Penance", in *Chaucer: The Canterbury Tales*, ed. Ellis. London and New York: Longman: pp. 169–88

Pearsall, Derek, ed. (1999). *Chaucer to Spenser: An Anthology of Writings in English 1375–1575*. Oxford: Blackwell

Pinti, Daniel J. (1996). "Teaching Chaucer through the Fifteenth Century", *Exemplaria* (Teaching Chaucer in the 90s), 8.2: 507–11

Portch, Stephen R. (1980). "A New Route Down Pilgrims' Way: Teaching Chaucer to Nonmajors", in *Approaches*, ed. Gibaldi. New York: The Modern Language Association of America: pp. 116–20

Ramsden, Paul (1992). *Learning to Teach in Higher Education*. London and New York: Routledge

Reasons, Saxon G., Kevin Valadares, & Michael Slavkin (2005). "Questioning the Hybrid Model: Student Outcomes in Different Course Formats", *Journal of Asynchronous Learning Networks*: http://www.sloan-c.org/publications/jaln/v9n1/v9n1_reasons.asp#reasons5

Remley, Paul (1996). "Questions of Subjectivity and Ideology in the Production of an Electronic Text of the *Canterbury Tales*", *Exemplaria* (Teaching Chaucer in the 90s), 8.2: 479–84

Richmond, Velma Bourgeois (1996). "Teaching Chaucer in a Small Catholic Liberal Arts College", *Exemplaria* (Teaching Chaucer in the 90s), 8.2: 495–505

Robertson Jr, D. W. (1962). *A Preface to Chaucer*. Princeton, NJ: Princeton University Press

Robertson, Kellie (2002). "Laboring in the God of Love's Garden: Chaucer's Prologue to *The Legend of Good Women*", *Studies in the Age of Chaucer*, 24: 115–47

Robinson, Peter, ed. (1996). *The Wife of Bath's* Prologue on CD-ROM. Cambridge: Cambridge University Press

———. ed. (2004). *The Miller's Tale* on CD-ROM. Leicester: Scholarly Digital Editions

Rose, Christine, ed. (1996). *Teaching Chaucer in the 90s: A Symposium, Exemplaria*, 8.2

Rubino, Antonia (2004). "Teaching Mixed-Ability Groups at Tertiary Level: The Case of Italian", *FULGOR: Flinders University Languages Group Online Review*, 2: 22–42

Ruggiers, Paul G., ed. (1979). *A Facsimile and Transcription of the Hengwrt Manuscript, with Variants from the Ellesmere Manuscript*. Oklahoma: Pilgrim Books

Ryan, John K., trans. (1960). *The Confessions of Saint Augustine*. Garden City, New York: Doubleday

Salvatori, Mariolina (1997). "Review: The Personal as Recitation", *College Composition and Communication*, 48: 566–83

Samuels, M. L. (1972). *Linguistic Evolution with Special Reference to English*. Cambridge: Cambridge University Press

Saunders, Corinne, ed. (2001). *Chaucer*. Oxford: Blackwell

Scanlon, Larry (1989). "The Authority of Fable: Allegory and Irony in the *Nun's Priest's Tale*", *Exemplaria*, 1: 43–68

Scase, Wendy (2002). "Tolkien, Philology, and The Reeve's Tale: Towards the Cultural Move in Middle English Studies", *Studies in the Age of Chaucer*, 24: 325–34

Schousboe, Steen. "Teaching Historical Linguistics": http://www.univie.ac.at/ Anglistik/hoe/pschousboe.htm

Semper, Philippa (2005). "Electronic Resources", in *Chaucer*, ed. Ellis. Oxford: Oxford University Press: pp. 607–19

Severs, J. Burke (1942). *The Literary Relationships of Chaucer's Clerk's Tale*, Yale Studies in English 96. New Haven: Yale University Press, repr. Hamden, CT: Archon Books, 1972

Simons, John & Brian Maidment (2004). "The Origins of the Reading Public, 1830–70", *English Subject Centre Newsletter*, 6: 25–7

Sinclair, Giles (February 1954). "Chaucer—Translated or Obliterated?", *College English*, 15.5: 272–7

Slavin, Robert E. (1990). *Cooperative Learning: Theory, Research and Practice*. Englewood Cliffs, NJ: Prentice-Hall

Smith, Jeremy (1996). *An Historical Study of English: Function, Form and Change*. London: Routledge

———. (2002). "Chaucer and the Invention of English", *Studies in the Age of Chaucer*, 24: 335–46

———. (forthcoming). "Middle English Language", in M. Corrie, ed. *The Blackwell Companion to Middle English Literature*. Oxford: Blackwell

Smith, Marc A. & Peter Kollock, eds (1999). *Communities in Cyberspace*. New York and London: Routledge

Solopova, Elizabeth, ed. (2000). *The General Prologue on CD-ROM*. Cambridge: Cambridge University Press

Squint, Kirstin L. (2002). "Non-Graded Group Work and Role-Playing: Empowering Students toward Critical Analysis", *Eureka Studies in Teaching Short Fiction*, 2: 103–6

Starko, Alane Jordan (1995). *Creativity in the Classroom: Schools of Curious Delight*. New York: Longman

Stubbs, Estelle, ed. (2000). *The Hengwrt Chaucer Digital Facsimile*. Leicester: Scholarly Digital Editions

Thompson, Ann (1978). *Shakespeare's Chaucer: A Study in Literary Origins*. New York: Barnes & Noble Books

Trigg, Stephanie (2002). "The New Medievalization of Chaucer", *Studies in the Age of Chaucer*, 24: 347–54

White, Edward M. (2001). "The Opening of the Modern Era of Writing Assessment: A Narrative", *College English*, 63: 306–20

Wiersema, Nico (2000). "How Does Collaborative Learning Actually Work in a Classroom and How Do Students React to It? A Brief Reflection": http://www.city.londonmet.ac.uk/deliberations/collaborativelearning/wiersema.html

Williams, Raymond (1977). *Marxism and Literature*. Oxford: Oxford University Press

Wolfe, Christopher R., ed. (2001). *Learning and Teaching on the World Wide Web*. San Diego, CA: Academic Press

Yancey, Kathleen Blake (1999). "Looking Back as We Look Forward: Historicizing Writing Assessment", *College Composition and Communication*, 50: 483–503

Zieman, Katherine (1997). "Chaucer's Voys.", *Representations*, 60: 70–91

Suggestions for Further Reading

Allen, Mark (2005). "Printed Resources", in *Chaucer*, ed. Ellis. Oxford: Oxford University Press: pp. 595–606

Alpay, Esat (2005). "Group Dynamic Processes in Email Groups", *Active Learning in Higher Education*, 6.1: 7–16

Andrew, Malcolm (2005). "Translations", in *Chaucer*, ed. Ellis. Oxford: Oxford University Press: pp. 544–59

Beidler, Peter G. (1985). "Chaucer and the Trots: What to Do About those Modern English Translations", *Chaucer Review*, 19: 290–301

Cartwright, Phillip (1999). *Designing and Producing Media-Based Training*. Boston and Oxford: Focal Press

Chin, Paul (2004). *Using C and IT to Support Teaching*. London and New York: RoutledgeFalmer

Cohen, Elizabeth G. (1986 and 1994). *Designing Groupwork: Strategies for the Heterogeneous Classroom*. New York: Teachers College Press

Collette, Carolyn (2002). "Afterlife", in *Companion*, ed. Brown. Oxford: Blackwell: pp. 8–22

Coote, Lesley & Brian Levy (2003). " 'The Middle Ages Go to the Movies': Medieval Texts, Medievalism and E-Learning", *Studies in Medieval and Renaissance Teaching*, 10: 25–49

Copeland, Rita (1991). *Rhetoric, Hermeneutics and Translation in the Middle Ages*. Cambridge: Cambridge University Press

Dalke, Anne French (2002). *Teaching to Learn / Learning to Teach: Meditations on the Classroom*. New York: Peter Lang Publishing, Inc.

Ellis, V. & A. Loveless, eds. (2001). *ICT, Pedagogy and the Curriculum: Subject to Change*. London and New York: RoutledgeFalmer

Gibbs, G., S. Habeshaw & T. Habeshaw (1987). *53 Interesting Ways to Assess Your Students*. Bristol: Technical and Educational Service

Goodman, Paul S. (1986). *Designing Effective Work Groups*, 1st edn. San Francisco: Jossey-Bass

Harty, Kevin J. (2005). "Chaucer in Performance", in *Chaucer*, ed. Ellis. Oxford: Oxford University Press: pp. 560–75

"Internet Resources in English" http://www.humbul.ac.uk/english/booklet/

Katz, Joseph & Mildred Henry (1993). *Turning Professors into Teachers: A New Approach to Faculty Development and Student Learning*. Phoenix, AZ: American Council on Education and Oryx Press

Lockwood, Anne Turnbaugh (1993). "Multiple Intelligences in Action ('The MI Provocation' and 'The MI Key')", *Journal of Research and the Classroom*, 4: 1–12

McAlpine, Lynn (2004). "Designing Learning As Well As Teaching: A Research-based Model for Instruction that Emphasises Learner Practice", *Active Learning in Higher Education*, 5.2: 119–34

McDermott, John J. (December 1975). "Teaching Students to Read Chaucer Aloud", *College English*, 37.4: 402–4

Sadlek, Gregory M. (Fall 2000). "Visualizing Chaucer's Pilgrim Society: Using Sociograms to Teach the 'General Prologue' of *The Canterbury Tales*", *Studies in Medieval and Renaissance Teaching*, 8.2: 77–97

Slavin, Robert E. (1990). *Cooperative Learning: Theory, Research and Practice.* Englewood Cliffs, NJ: Prentice-Hall

Topping, K. J. (1996). "The Effectiveness of Peer Tutoring in Further and Higher Education: A Typology and Review of the Literature", *Higher Education*, 32: 321–45

Weimer, Maryellen (2002). *Learner-Centered Teaching: Five Key Changes to Practice.* San Francisco: Jossy-Bass

Wolfe, Christopher R., ed. (2001). *Learning and Teaching on the World Wide Web.* San Diego, CA: Academic Press

For more information/resources on teaching English (both print and web-based) please go to the following link on the English Subject Centre web site:

http://www.english.heacademy.ac.uk/explore/resources/scholarship/publication.php

Web Resources

Primary texts on-line

Caxton's Canterbury Tales: The British Library Copies
  http://www.bl.uk/treasures/caxton/homepage.html
Chaucer MetaPage Listing: Texts of Chaucer's Works On-line
  http://www.unc.edu/depts/chaucer/chtexts.htm
Chaucertext: An On-line Archive for Electronic Chaucer Scholarship
  http://www.winthrop.edu/chaucertext/
Corpus of Middle English Verse and Prose
  http://www.hti.umich.edu/c/cme/
Edwin Duncan: An Electronic Edition of the "General Prologue" to Geoffrey
  Chaucer's "Canterbury Tales"
  http://www.towson.edu/~duncan/chaucer/
Electronic Literature Foundation: The Canterbury Tales
  http://hosting.uaa.alaska.edu/afdtk/ect_main.htm
The Canterbury Tales Project
  http://www.ucalgary.ca/~scriptor/chaucer/rob.html
The Internet Medieval Sourcebook
  http://www.fordham.edu/HALSALL/sbook.html
University of Virginia Electronic Text Centre
  http://etext.lib.virginia.edu/collections/languages/english/
  mideng.browse.html

Language resources

A Basic Chaucer Glossary
  http://www.towson.edu/~duncan/glossary.html
Chaucer MetaPage Audio Files
  http://academics.vmi.edu/english/audio/audio_index.html
The Chaucer Studio
  http://english.byu.edu/chaucer/
Melinda Menzer, The Great Vowel Shift
  http://facweb.furman.edu/~mmenzer/gvs/
Middle English Glossarial Database
  http://www.hti.umich.edu/g/gloss/
The *Middle English Dictionary* On-line
  http://ets.umdl.umich.edu/m/med/

Information on historical contexts

Late Medieval Maps 1300–1500
  http://www.henry-davis.com/MAPS/LMwebpages/LM1.html

Luminarium Additional Sources for Medieval England
  http://www.luminarium.org/medlit/medresource.htm
The Harvard Geoffrey Chaucer Page
  http://www.courses.fas.harvard.edu/~chaucer/
TimeRef Medieval History Timelines
  http://www.btinternet.com/~timeref/

Discussion lists and forums

Archives of the Chaucer Discussion Group
  http://www.towson.edu/~duncan/acalists.html
The New Chaucer Society
  http://www.artsci.wustl.edu/~chaucer/

Portals and metapages

Baragona's Chaucer Page
  http://academics.vmi.edu/english/chaucer.html
geoffreychaucer.org
  http://geoffreychaucer.org/
Hanley's Chaucer Scriptorium
  http://www.wsu.edu/~hanly/chaucer/chaucer.html
Humbul Humanities Hub (English Studies)
  http://www.humbul.ac.uk/english/
Jack Lynch, Literary Resources: Medieval
  http://andromeda.rutgers.edu/~jlynch/Lit/medieval.html
The Labyrinth: Resources for Medieval Studies
  http://www.georgetown.edu/labyrinth/
Luminarium Geoffrey Chaucer Page
  http://www.luminarium.org/lumina.htm
The Chaucer MetaPage
  http://www.unc.edu/depts/chaucer/
The ORB (Online Reference Book for Medieval Studies)
  http://the-orb.net/

Bibliographies

On-Line Chaucer Bibliography
  http://www.unc.edu/depts/chaucer/chbib.htm
The Essential Chaucer (Annotated Bibliography of Chaucer Studies 1900–84)
  http://colfa.utsa.edu/chaucer/
The Chaucer Review: An Indexed Bibliography Vols. 1–30
  http://www3.baylor.edu/~Chaucer_Bibliography/

Index